REV. JŌSHŌ ADRIAN CIREA

THE FOUR PROFOUND THOUGHTS WHICH TURN THE MIND TOWARDS AMIDA DHARMA

Dharma Lion Publications

CRAIOVA, 2018

Copyright © Adrian Gheorghe Cîrlea

All rights reserved. No part of this book may be reproduced without prior written permission from the author.

Rev. Jōshō Adrian Cîrlea (Adrian Gheorghe Cîrlea) is the representative of Jodo Shinshu Buddhist Community from Romania, founder of Tariki Dojo and Amidaji Temple. He is also the author of *The Path of Acceptance – Commentary on Tannisho*, Dharma Lion, 2011, *Jodo Shinshu Buddhist Teachings*, Dharma Lion, 2012, *The 48 Vows of Amida Buddha*, Dharma Lion, 2013, *The True Teaching on Amida Buddha and His Pure Land*, Dharma Lion, 2015

Cîrlea Gheorghe Adrian
Oficiul Postal 3, Ghiseul Postal 3
Casuta postala 615
Cod poştal (postal code) 200900
Craiova, judet Dolj
Romania

phone: 0745038390
e-mail: josho_adrian@yahoo.com
skype id: josho_adrian
Website: www.amida-ji-retreat-temple-romania.blogspot.com

I dedicate this book to Andreea Călugărița, Bruce Barbour, Catalin Halmageanu, Chanvibol Kit, Costel Golfin, Cristian Anton, C.Y. Wang, Cheusa Wend, Eb Whipple, Cobi Chen, Janne Heikkila, Jim E, Gilli Kit, Judy Ng, Heng Ng, Hedy Ito, Jonathan Khor, Jufang Wong, Kenya-Lee Province, Kong Yim, Loh Khin Kok ,Phyllis Latham Stoner, William Richard Stoner, Mattias Wernstig, Neal Oldham, Shinkai Thais Campos, Sylvie Egrotti, Raymond Egrotti
Teh Phek Hong, Tamira Cîrlea, Yokusho Gheorghe Cîrlea, Gheorghe Cîrlea, Cristina Cîrlea, Constantin Iovan, Ioana Iovan, Valerie Whelan, Veronica Anghelescu, Waldik D L Souza and to all sentient beings in the ten directions. May they all reach the Pure Land of Amida Buddha and attain perfect Enlightenment.

TABLE OF CONTENTS

Foreword 6
Some general notions of Jodo Shinshu Buddhism 8
Preciousness of human birth 18
Impermanence and death 29
Karma - the law of cause and effect 39
Samsara is suffering 77
Concluding thoughts on the suffering of samsaric existence 179
The benefits of being born in the Pure Land of Amida Buddha 195
Concluding verses on the Four Profound Thoughts which turn the mind towards Amida Dharma 225

Foreword

The Four Profound Thoughts are basic teachings, something like a preliminary to any Buddhist path or practice. It has the effect of turning the mind towards the Buddha Dharma and should be a constant companion no matter if one is a beginner or an older follower. Sometimes they are reffered to as the Four Contemplations, the Four Understandings or the Four Reminders. Because in this book I explain them in the context of the Pure Land Dharma Gate of Jodo Shinshu (Amida Dharma), I decided to call them the Four Profound Thoughts which Turn the Mind Towards the Amida Dharma. These Profound Thoughts are:

1. Preciousness of human birth
2. Impermanence and death
3. Karma - the law of cause and effect
4. Samsara is suffering

If one contemplates, understands and never forgets these four, then one is a serious follower of Shakyamuni Buddha and Amida Buddha. Such a contemplation, understanding and remembering is not something special, but a simple knowing that our situation is defined by the above four truths. My goal in writing these teachings is to use the awarenes they provide to convince my Dharma friends of the importance of taking refuge in Amida Buddha and aspire to be born in His Pure Land. I hope that the passages I carefully chose from various sacred texts and ancient masters, as well as my explanations, will have a big impact on them not only at the intelectual level, but also at deeper, more emotional one.

Amida Dharma is not a mere object of study, but the most important medicine ever offered to sentient beings. Life in human form, impermanence and death, the law of karma and the sufferings of samsara are serious business and should be treated with utmost seriousness. This is why reading this book should not only be a process of accumulating informations, but also engaging the reader into a profound contemplation on these four truths.

Read and think deeply to the rare chance you have to be born in human form. Read and become aware of your own impermanence. Read and let yourself be shocked by the implacable law of karma and the various sufferings of samsaric existence. Read and realize you have no other choice but to take refuge in Amida Buddha and aspire to be born in His safe Enlightened realm.

Namo Amida Bu

Jōshō Adrian Cîrlea
November, 2561 Buddhist Era (2017 C.E.)
Amidaji Temple

Some general notions of Jodo Shinshu Buddhism

Before I treat the topic of this book I invite the reader to become familiar with some general notions of Jodo Shinshu Buddhism, so that it will be easier for him to understand the teachings presented here.

1) Samsara and Nirvana (Budhahood/Enlightenment)
Samsara is the cycle of repeated births and deaths. Because it is the effect of personal and collective (inter-related) karma[1] of unenlightened beings[2], it has no other creator[3] than our own delusions, attachments and cravings. There are many samsaric states of existence, among which we mention, hells, hungry ghosts, animals, humans, asuras or fighting spirits and gods. All beings are born, die, and are reborn again in those respective realms due to their karma, and their existence is accompanied by different types of suffering, obscurations and delusions.

The goal of the Buddha Path is to escape from Samsara and attain the state of Buddhahood or Nirvana[4]/Perfect

---

[1] Read the chapter "General explanations of being, karma and rebirth" from *The True Teaching on Amida Buddha and His Pure Land*, by Josho Adrian Cirlea, Dharma Lion Publications, Craiova, 2015, p 14

[2] Read the chapter "Some buddhist explanations of the origin and existence of the universe" from *The True Teaching on Amida Buddha and His Pure Land*, p 31.

[3] Read the chapter, "There is no creator God in the Buddha Dharma" from *The True Teaching on Amida Buddha and His Pure Land*, p 18

[4] Nirvana comes from the verb „nirv" – „to extinguish", and is wrongly understood by many as becoming nothingness. However,

Enlightenment. This is the highest freedom and happiness which does not depend on any cause and condition, and it is the potential inherent in all sentient beings, no matter how low they are now on the scale of spiritual evolution. Simply stated, just like all seeds have the natural potential to become trees, all sentient beings have the natural potential to become Buddhas, that is, to awaken to their own Buddha nature. This is what is meant in Buddhism by "all beings have Buddha nature"[5]. Beyond the various layers of our delusory personality, the Buddha nature is the true reality, uncreated and indestructbile, the treasure hidden in every one of us. When it's discovered, the causes of suffering and repeteaded births and deaths are anihilated and the one who attained it becomes himself a savior and guide of all beings that are still caught in the slavery of samsara.

The state of Nirvana or Buddhahood is supreme in the universe. All those who attain it are called Buddhas. No gods, spirits or divine figures of various religions are superiors to Buddhas, and no religion or spiritual path equals the teaching of the Buddha. This is exactly why we, as Buddhist disciples, take refuge only in the Buddha, His Dharma and the community of His true followers (Sangha), and why we do not worship, nor

---

„Nirvana" means to extinguish the flame of blind passions and illusions and to awake to the true reality or Buddha nature which all beings possess. In the Jodo Shinshu school, the state of Nirvana or Buddhahood is to be attained in the moment of birth in the Pure Land of Amida, after death. The term "Nirvana" is eccuivalent to "Perfect Enlightenment", "Buddha nature", "Buddhahood", etc.
[5] Read the chapter "Two questions on Buddha nature and samsara" from *The True Teaching on Amida Buddha and His Pure Land*, p 51.

depend on any religious figure outside the Buddha Dharma[6].

Samsara is often depicted in the sacred texts as a collective dream, while samsaric (unenlightened) beings are described as people who are asleep in the long night of ignorance. The Buddhas, who are the only Awakened/Enlightened Persons (the word "Buddha" means "The Awakened One"), have Infinite Wisdom and Infinite Compassion and so they always act as awakeners of others. The collection of teachings and practices by which the Buddhas try to awake or help unenlightened sentient beings is called the Buddha Dharma.

2) Shakyamuni Buddha and His teaching on Amida Buddha's salvation

According to the Buddha Dharma, the human history, as we know it, is only a very small fraction of the endless and inconceivable time of the universe. This means that many world systems and beings living in them had existed before the appearance of this earth and will continue to exist after its dissapearance. Thus, in the begingless past a great number of Buddhas appeared in various worlds and will continue to appear in the never ending future. However, the Enlightened Person who taught the Buddha Dharma during our present human history was Shakyamuni Buddha.

---

[6] Read the chapter, "Those who believe in a creator God cannot have true faith in Amida Buddha", from *The True Teaching on Amida Buddha and His Pure Land*, by Josho Adrian Cirlea, Dharma Lion Publications, Craiova, 2015, p 54

In His long life, Shakyamuni met many people of various spiritual capacities and conditions, and He taught many discourses. These discourses, which are called sutras, were transmitted to future generations by His closest disciples through various means, including oral transmission or through special states of mind called Samadhi, until they were finaly put into written form.

Different Buddhist schools were formed based on various sutras (discourses). Our Jodo Shinshu school was formed based on of the Three Pure Land Sutras as they were explained by Shinran Shonin (1173-1262), the Founding Master. These sutras are: *The Sutra of the Buddha of Immeasurable Life* (Bussetsu Muryoju Kyo), *The Sutra of Contemplation of the Buddha of Immeasurable Life (Bussetsu Kammuryoju Kyo)* and *The Smaller Sutra on Amida Buddha (Bussetsu Amida Kyo)*.

Especially, the *Sutra of the Buddha of Immeasurable Life* (or *Larger Sutra*) was considered by Shinran Shonin to be the most important teaching of Shakyamuni Buddha's lifetime, and the main reason for His appearance in our world[7]. In this sutra He told the story of Amida Buddha and His Pure Land[8], encouraging all beings to entrust to Him and wish to be born there.

---

[7] Read the chapter "The purpose of Shakyamuni's coming to this world" from *Jodo Shinshu Buddhist Teachings,* by Josho Adrian Cirlea, Dharma Lion Publications, Craiova, 2012, p32.

[8] Read the chapter "The story of Amida Buddha as told by Shakyamuni Buddha" from *The True Teaching on Amida Buddha and His Pure Land*, by Josho Adrian Cirlea, Dharma Lion Publications, Craiova, 2015, p. 66

Unlike Shakyamuni, Amida is not a historical figure, but a transcendent Buddha who attained Enlightenment many eons ago in the distant past[9]. However, He is as real as Shakyamuni or any Buddha of any time as all Buddhas remain forever active in the salvation of sentient beings.

The specific characteristic of Amida Buddha is that He made 48 Vows for the salvation of all sentient beings, and manifested a real enlightened place called the Pure Land (Sukhavati). Some of the vows describe His special characteristics as a Buddha (12th Vow, and 13th Vow), others describe the qualities of the Pure Land (31st Vow and 32nd Vow), while others explain how sentient beings can be born there after death and how they will live or behave after arriving there.
Among His vows, the 18th or the Primal Vow is considered to be the most important. In it, He promised that He will bring to His Pure Land all beings who entrust to Him, say His Name in faith and wish to be born there. Other vows also promise that those born in His Pure Land through the gate of the Primal Vow will attain Nirvana (11th Vow) and then come back to the Samsaric

---

[9] Read the chapters "About Amida Buddha and His Pure Land" from *Jodo Shinshu Buddhist Teachings,* by Josho Adrian Cirlea, Dharma Lion Publications, Craiova, 2012, p 20 and "The Doctrine of the Three Buddha Bodies of Amida Buddha", from *The True Teaching on Amida Buddha and His Pure Land*, by Josho Adrian Cirlea, Dharma Lion Publications, Craiova, 2015, p. 88

realms, in various forms, to save other beings (22nd Vow)[10].

As already explained at the begining of this introduction, the Samsaric environment in which we now live is the effect of our karma and the inter-related karma (collective karma) of all unenlightened beings. This impure common karma gave rise to an impure environment which also influences us and in which it is hard to have a true spiritual evolution. We ourselves are sick, our fellow beings are sick and the environment is also sick. This is why we are urged to aspire to be born after death, in the Pure Land. This land is the healthy enlightened realm of Amida Buddha, a suitable environment which is not the product of evil karma, blind passions and attachements, but of His pure karmic merits. Once born in such a sane environment our insanity is cured instantly, our delusions are naturally melt like ice meeting fire, and our true enlightened nature (Buddha nature) will reveal itself.

According to the Buddha Dharma, Samsaric or unenlightened beings are like seeds dropped in an infertile soil. Although the potentiality of any seed is to become a tree, if you place it in a poor soil, devoid of any good nutrients, and in the presence of various bad weeds, the seed will not grow. Just like the seed, the potentiality of any being is to become a Buddha, but because we live in this samsaric world, itself the effect

---

[10] For a complete explanation of all the 48 Vows of Amida Buddha see *The 48 Vows of Amida Buddha*, by Josho Adrian Cirlea, Dharma Lion Publications, Craiova, 2013.

and echo of our own evil karma, we cannot grow and transform ourselves into Buddhas. This is exactly why we need to let Amida take us to His Pure Land[11]. That Land is the best soil for seeds like us to quickly develop their natural potential and become Buddhas. Unlike the various Samsaric planes of existence, the Pure Land is the soil (realm) of Enlightenment, the perfect garden manifested by Amida Buddha where everything is conducive to Enlightenment. So, we should all simply entrust to Him and wish to be planted/reborn there, where by receiving all the necesary nutrients and not being obstructed by any bad weeds, we'll naturally transform ourselves into Trees of Enlightenment.

3) The Faith (Shinjin) and Nembutsu of the Primal Vow

Shinran Shonin often insisted in his teaching that we must be in accord with the Primal Vow.

To be in accord with the Primal Vow means that we accept it as being true and effective in saving us, that we entrust to Amida Buddha, say His Name in faith and wish to be born in His Land.

To accept that the Primal Vow is true and effective also means that the elements of this Vow are true and real. Which are these elements? They are Amida Buddha and His Pure Land. Only in relation with this Buddha and His Pure Land there is a faith, a saying of the Name and a wish to be born. Faith in whom? It is faith in Amida.

---

[11] Read the chapter "The two aspects of the Pure Land" from *The True Teaching on Amida Buddha and His Pure Land*, by Josho Adrian Cirlea, Dharma Lion Publications, Craiova, 2015, p. 101

Saying the Name of whom? Saying the Name of Amida. Wishing to be born in whose land? Wishing to be born in Amida's Land.

If we have faith in someone, then it means we are sure beyond any doubt that he is reliable and that he will keep his promise. Also to believe in someone's promise means that we accept his existence, too. Promises can be made by living persons, in our case by a living, existing Amida Buddha, not by material objects or fictional characters[12]. So, only if we accept the actual existence of Amida Buddha and of His Pure Land, we can have a genuine faith in Him, say His Name and wish to be born there. Because Amida Buddha and His Pure Land are true and real, His Primal Vow, in which He urges us to entrust to Him, say His Name and wish to go there, is itself true and real. We are not speaking here about an empty promise made by an unenlightened person, or by a fictional character in a fantasy book, but about the promise of a real Buddha, the fully Enlightened One called Amida. Because He exists and He is a Buddha, then it means He is reliable and we can let Him carry us to His Pure Land.

When one has faith (shinjin), one is convinced that Amida Buddha and His Pure Land exists, and that the Promise He made in His Primal Vow is true, so he/she

---

[12] Read the chapters, "Those who deny the existence of Amida don't have shinjin" from *Jodo Shinshu Buddhist Teachings,* by Josho Adrian Cirlea, Dharma Lion Publications, Craiova, 2012, p 186 and "The karmic consequence of denying the trancendent reality of Amida Buddha and His Pure Land" from *The True Teaching on Amida Buddha and His Pure Land*, by Josho Adrian Cirlea, Dharma Lion Publications, Craiova, 2015, p. 109

simply entrusts to this Buddha and wishes to go to His Pure Land after death. Saying Namo Amida Butsu (Nembutsu) often or seldom means exactly this – "I entrust to Amida Buddha/I take refuge in Amida Buddha and I wish to go to His Pure Land". It also means, "Thank you Amida Buddha for saving me and taking me to your Pure Land at the end of this physical body". "Namo" from "Namo Amida Butsu[13]", means "homage to", which expresses gratitude and also "to take refuge" which expresses faith (shinjin). "Butsu" or "Bu" (if you like to recite it as "Namo Amida Bu"), means "Buddha".

In the exact moment we entrust to Amida Buddha, we enter the stage of non-retrogression, that is, no matter what happens to us, we are assured of birth in the Pure Land. Just like all rivers flow to the ocean, all beings who entrust to Amida will inevitably be born in His Pure Land after death. Once we put our faith in Amida, nothing constitutes an obstacle to birth there, not even our illusion or evil karma. This is why the stage is called, "non-retrogression."

*

There is no special advice to give on how to say the Nembutsu, other than just say it. So, let us enjoy Amida Buddha's Name and say it anytime we like, in whatever circumstances we are. Amida wants us to enjoy His Name freely and without worry. This Name does not require any initiation, empowerment or special states of

---

[13] Namo Amida Butsu, Namo Amida Bu, or Namandabu is the same.

mind[14]. Thus, no matter if we feel good or bad, if we are calm or have an agitated mind, we just say the Name. When we say the Name we do not take refuge in our own mind, in the thoughts that appear in it, in our feelings or ideas, but in Amida Buddha who is outside of our mind.

The reason why in our Jodo Shinshu school it is taught that although we say the Nembutsu with our lips, it is not "our practice", is because the Name of Amida does not belong to us, and so, it is not improved or damaged by anything, good or bad, that we have in our personality. The Name is the manifestation of Amida and it works because of Amida. We do not provide anything to the Name to make it effective. While other Pure Land schools focus on the person saying the Name and are busy teaching their followers to have a good state of mind when saying it, our Jodo Shinshu school focuses on Amida and His Power to save. Here we just let Amida save us. When we, Jodo Shinshu followers, say the Name we simply express this faith and we say, "thank you, Amida Buddha".

---

[14] Read the chapter "Faith is simple, nothing special" from *Jodo Shinshu Buddhist Teachings,* by Josho Adrian Cirlea, Dharma Lion Publications, Craiova, 2012, p 88.

Preciousness of human birth

"This free and well-favoured human form is difficult to obtain.
Now that you have the chance to realize the full human potential,
If you don't make good use of this opportunity,
How could you possibly expect to have such a chance again?"[15]

The first thought that turns the mind toward the Buddha Dharma is the preciousness of human birth and the importance of using it well for escaping samsara. But what is so special about birth in human form? There are a few elements here. First, **the human birth is extremely rare**. Second, **human birth is a favorable balance between pain and pleasure which makes listening and devoting to the Dharma easier**.
To make us realize how rare is birth in human form Shakyamuni Buddha told the following parable from the *Chiggala Sutra*:

"'Monks, suppose that this great earth were totally covered with water, and a man were to toss a yoke with a single hole there. A wind from the east would push it west, a wind from the west would push it east. A wind from the north would push it south, a wind from the south would push it north. And suppose a blind sea-turtle were there. It would come to the surface once every one hundred years. Now what do you think: would that blind

---

[15] *Bodhicharyavatara.*

sea-turtle, coming to the surface once every one hundred years, stick his neck into the yoke with a single hole?'

'It would be a sheer coincidence, Lord, that the blind sea-turtle, coming to the surface once every one hundred years, would stick his neck into the yoke with a single hole.'
'And just so, it is very, very rare that one attains the human state.'"[16]

Here is another suggestive parable:

"Then the Blessed One, picking up a little bit of dust with the tip of His fingernail, said to the monks, 'What do you think, monks? Which is greater: the little bit of dust I have picked up with the tip of my fingernail, or the great earth?'
'The great earth is far greater, lord. The little bit of dust the Blessed One has picked up with the tip of His fingernail is next to nothing. It doesn't even count. It's no comparison. It's not even a fraction, this little bit of dust the Blessed One has picked up with the tip of His fingernail, when compared with the great earth.'
'In the same way, monks, few are the beings who, on passing away from the human realm, are reborn among human beings. Far more are the beings who, on passing

---

[16] Adaptation after *Chiggala Sutta: The Hole* (SN 56.48), translated from the Pali by Thanissaro Bhikkhu. Access to Insight (Legacy Edition), 1 July 2010, http://www.accesstoinsight.org/tipitaka/sn/sn56/sn56.048.than.html

away from the human realm, are reborn in hell.' [...]

Then the Blessed One, picking up a little bit of dust with the tip of his fingernail, said to the monks, 'What do you think, monks? Which is greater: the little bit of dust I have picked up with the tip of my fingernail, or the great earth?'
'The great earth is far greater, lord. The little bit of dust the Blessed One has picked up with the tip of His fingernail is next to nothing. It doesn't even count. It's no comparison. It's not even a fraction, this little bit of dust the Blessed One has picked up with the tip of His fingernail, when compared with the great earth.'
'In the same way, monks, few are the beings who, on passing away from the human realm, are reborn among human beings. Far more are the beings who, on passing away from the human realm, are reborn in the animal womb... in the domain of the hungry ghosts.'

... 'In the same way, monks, few are the beings who, on passing away from the human realm, are reborn among devas. Far more are the beings who, on passing away from the human realm, are reborn in hell... in the animal womb... in the domain of the hungry ghosts.'

... 'In the same way, monks, few are the beings who, on passing away from the deva realm, are reborn among devas. Far more are the beings who, on passing away from the deva realm, are reborn in hell... in the animal womb... in the domain of the hungry ghosts.'

... 'In the same way, monks, few are the beings who, on passing away from the deva realm, are reborn among human beings. Far more are the beings who, on passing away from the deva realm, are reborn in hell... in the animal womb... in the domain of the hungry ghosts'''.[17]

As we have seen in the above two quotes, very few beings can be reborn again in human form after they die, and the number of non-human beings is far more numerous than humans. We can easily realise this by comparing the insects on this planet with the humans. Even if we are now more than seven bilion people, insects will always be more numerous than us. Also, the lower states of existence (hells, the realm of hungry spirits and animals) receive more beings than our human plane. When people focus on hate motivated activities they easily plant a karmic connection with the hell realm, thus being born after death in one of the hells. In the same way, its easier to let onself dominated by greed or avarice and open the gate to the hungry spirits or to become dominated by instincts and be reborn in animal form, than to plant the good karmic seeds of human rebirth.

Some people wrongly assert that once born a human one will stay a human or continue to evolve until Nirvana or

---

[17] *Pansu Suttas: Dust* (SN 56.102-113), translated from the Pali by Thanissaro Bhikkhu. Access to Insight (Legacy Edition), 10 December 2011, http://www.accesstoinsight.org/tipitaka/sn/sn56/sn56.102-113.than.html

Enlightenment is attained. Thus, they think that spiritual evolution is a straight line from which one cannot retrogress. However, that is a grave delusion. What they do in fact, is lying to themselves by projecting their own wishes for security, and creating a "safety zone" for their fearful minds. In truth, when we look at many of our human beings, and even at ourselves, we see that very often feelings of hate, pride, jealousy, avarice, and so on, are surfacing the waves of our minds. Some human beings behave like animals when it comes to lust, forgetting everything for some hours of pleasure, even sacrificing large amounts of money for this or for eating and drinking. Their minds are focused almost entirely on sex, food and drink, so how do these people resemble human beings? Some are constantly engaged in cruel behavior, killing or torturing other beings, while others work only to amass wealth without giving a single coin to those in need. How do all these people with such perverted conscience can still be considered humans? **While their bodies are still in the human realm, their mind-stream already started to resemble those of animals, hell dwellers or hungry spirits, so when their karmic cause for being in the human realm is exhausted, their conscience will naturaly and automatically enter a form (body) and world with which they resonate.** Its not wrong to say that a human behaving like a pig will one day become a pig and live among pigs.

Also, the pain which exist in the lower realms, especially in the hells or preta (hungry spirits) realm is too great, while in the asura (demi-gods) and gods realms the pleasure is too high and intoxicating. In both cases is very hard or even impossible to think to the Dharma.

Just imagine you have very high fever and diarrhea every day, and I call you to the temple. Could you really come? Could you come here to sit normaly and listen with a clear mind? Now imagine that pain multiplied bilions of times, with your body being pierced by extreme pain, burnt constantly, boiled, freezed in antarctic cold or feeling excruciating hunger and thirst like beings born in the hells or preta states. Also imagine yourself an animal, being hunted or raised for your meat, constantly living in fear of being killed or always pressured to hunt others to eat. Imagine you are under the total control of your instincts and with the conscience of a mere child. How can you really focus on understanding and practicing the Dharma in that state?

Now imagine that after many years of destitution you are spending one week with the most beautiful woman in the world, eating the best food, drinking the best wine and staying in an expansive resort made just for you, where everything your heart desires is provided. Think that I call you to the temple to hear the Dharma in the middle of that week. Will you really be able come? Now imagine that pleasure multiplied bilions of time and lasting for thousands of thousands of years, intoxicating your body and mind. How easy is to forget the Dharma in such a godly condition, and how painful will be when that god will approach his life's end, as the karmic energy which propeled him into that state is exhausted and he will fall again in the lower states fo existence.

We know from the sacred texts that there are some gods or even powerful spirits who practice the Dharma, acting as mundane protectors of the teaching and disciples, but those who fall prey to the immense pleasures of their state of existence are far more numerous, and so, the Dharma remains mainly unpracticed in the higher realms. Contrary to the lower or higher states of existence, in the human realm pain and happiness is balanced. Here there is not so much suffering like in the hells, pretas and animal realms, and not so much intoxicating happiness and pleasure like in the realms of asuras and gods.

But why is human life so hard to obtain? It is because one needs a good karmic cause for that. Birth in human form comes as the effect of a great amount of merit accumulated in past lives through effort at observing the precepts and altruistic attitude of mind to benefit others. So, it means that some times in our former existences we cultivated such merits, and due to a combination of those causes and favorable conditions we were now born as humans. However, we also planted and are now planting many other types of karma, some being evil or egocentric, which also need to manifest and generate next rebirths. Thus, karma is not of a single colour or type, but many, and combines itself in endless variations of good, evil or neutral causes, and so we never know what might manifest at the end of this present life or during it. Because we are not certain of our future rebirth, we must do our best with this human life to enter the stage of non-retrogression[18], that is, of those assured of birth in the Pure Land through faith in Amida Buddha.

We use the words "preciousness of human birth", but this does not mean that any life in human form is auspicious from the Buddhist point of view. To be born in a human body but spending your entire life focused only on eating, drinking, satisfiying your sensual desires, or looking for fame and wealth without giving any thought to the Dharma cannot be considered an auspicious or precious human life. On the contrary, its a waste of the rare opportunity to be born in human form. Also, being physically or mentaly incapacitated (incomplete faculties) so that one cannot hear and understand the Dharma, living in a place without the conditions of meeting the Dharma or embracing wrong views and non-Buddhist religions cannot be considered an auspicious or precious human life.

It is said **that there are eight freedoms and ten advantages of a really precious human life, that is, of a human life dedicated to the Dharma.** The eight freedoms are the freedom from the eight states where there is almost no opportunity to practice the Dharma: 1) the state of hell, 2) preta, 3) animals, 4) long-living gods,

---

[18] In the exact moment we entrust to Amida Buddha, we enter the stage of non-retrogression, that is, no matter what happens to us, we are assured of birth in the Pure Land. Just like all rivers flow to the ocean, all beings who entrust to Amida will inevitably be born in His Pure Land after death. Once we put our faith in Amida, nothing constitutes an obstacle to birth there, not even our evil karma. This is why the stage is called, "non-retrogression."

5) lands or countries where there is no Dharma, 6) incomplete faculties, 7) freedom from wrong views and 8) freedom from a state of existence or universe where the Buddha has not come.

As I explained earlier, if you were born in the lower realms (hells, preta, animals) the suffering would be unbearable and you would suffer from intense heat, cold, hunger, thirst, or being hunted down and killed for meat, and if you were born in he higher realms of existence (asuras and gods) you would be too much intoxicated with pleasures and enjoyable distractions. Incomplete faculties means to be physically or mentaly incapacitated, and so understanding the Dharma would be very much limited or even impossible. Also being sane but embracing wrong views like nihilism, eternalism - belief in a supreme god or in other divine figures outside Buddhism, denying the actual and literal existence of Amida Buddha and His Pure Land, are insurmontable obstacles in your Dharma practice and in fulfilling your life in human form. Last but not least, to be born a human in a universe or world where the Buddha has not come is futile because you could not meet the Dharma to make your life meaningful. It's the same with living in a country where there is no opportunity to meet the Dharma.

The ten advantages are: 1) a Buddha has come in the world and 2) He has taught the Dharma, 3) the Dharma teachings have survived, 4) there are followers of the Dharma, 5) there are favourable conditions for listening the Dharma, 6) being born as a human, 7) being born in a place where the Dharma is available, 8) being born with the physical and mental faculties intact, 9) having a karmic predisposition to search for the meaning of life and spiritual fulfillment, 10) to have faith in the sutras or words of the Buddha.

In our case, Shakyamuni Buddha has come to this world and taught many Dharma gates, among which the teaching of Amida's unconditional salvation (Amida Dharma) of all sentient beings stands foremost. This Amida Dharma has been transmited by many masters, teachers and lay followers of past and present and we ourselves are now accepting it in faith. Also, even if there are many places where wrong views are taught, one can still find some temples or dojos where the true Amida Dharma is present. Enjoying our human life in a place where Amida Dharma is taught, we can listen to it with our hearing organs, understand it through our intelect, ask questions or discuss our doubts with others and eventually receive faith in our hearts.

Also, without feeling the need for spiritual search and fulfilement, we could not reach the most important moment of our life when we met Amida Dharma and entrusted ourselves to it. Even if some of us tried one or many religious paths until we discovered the Dharma and entrusted ourselves to it, **the fact that we were serious in our search** created more karmic causes which took us closer and closer to the true teaching about Amida Buddha.

One of the most important features of human life is that it lasts very little in comparison with the lifetime of gods, asuras and even some beings in the lower realms, also, it is not fixed. For example, Master Genshin described in his Ojoyoshu that, *"a hundred years of human life are equal in length to one day and night in the Heaven of the Thirty-three, and in this heaven life lasts a thousand years"* or that *"a hundred years of human life are equal in length to one day and night in the Heaven of the Thirty-Three Gods, and in this heaven life lasts a thousand years, but the length of life in the Heaven of the Thirty-Three gods is equivalent to only one day and night in this hell and here life lasts one thousand years."* Also, in other hells or gods realms life can last even a whole kalpa! In comparison with such beings who enjoy immense pleasure or excruciating pain, human life is extremely short and unpredictable, so we should do our best with what we have and focus on listening the Dharma and receive faith, thus entering the stage of non-retrogression and being sure this is our last life as samsaric beings.

*"It is rare to obtain human life,
And diffcult to encounter a Buddha in this world;
Hard it is to attain the wisdom of faith;
Once you have heard the Dharma, pursue it with diligence".*[19]

---

[19] Shinran Shonin, *Kyogyoshinsho – On Teaching, Practice, Faith, and Enlightenment*, translated by Hisao Inagaki, Numata Center for Buddhist Translation and Research, Kyoto, 2003, p. 13

Impermanence and death

*"This existence of ours is as transient as autumn clouds.
To watch the birth and death of beings is like looking at the movement of a dance.
A lifetime is like a flash of lightning in the sky,
Rushing by, like a torrent down a steep mountain".*[20]

Nothing that can be found in samsara lasts forever: the outer universe, the bodies of beings in various states of existence, the social status and wealth, our so called "spiritual achievements", etc.

The great world systems with their various realms and planets that appear due to collective karma of beings inhabiting them will disintegrate one day. Then, other worlds will be born and die again.[21] The long-living gods of higher states of existence know death too, just like any samsaric being. Rulers of vast celestial realms as well as rulers of humans will also die and their kingdoms will dissapear. Rich and poor, succesful people or losers, all will leave their present bodies and will not take with them any of their worldly achievements or failure. Death is indeed, the great equalizer:

*"Just as mountains of solid rock,
Massive, reaching to the sky,*

---

[20] Shakyamuni Buddha, *Lalitavistara Sutra*.
[21] See the chapter, "Some Buddhist explanations on the origin and existence of the universe" from my book, *The True Teaching on Amida Buddha and His Pure Land*, Dharma Lion Publications, Craiova, 2015, p 31.

Might draw together from all sides,
Crushing all in the four quarters -
So aging and death come
Rolling over living beings -

Warriors, brahmins, traders, hunters,
Outcasts and scavengers:
They spare none along the way
But come crushing everything.
There's no hope there for victory [against aging and death]
By elephant troops, chariots, and infantry.
One can't defeat them by subterfuge,
Or buy them off by means of wealth.

Therefore a person of wisdom here,
Out of regard for his own good,
Steadfast, should settle faith
In the Buddha, Dhamma, and Sangha[22]."[23]

As mentioned before, human life is very short in comparison with the lifetime of gods, asuras and even some beings in the lower realms and, it is not fixed.

---

[22] Read the chapter, "The Meaning of the Three Refuges in Jodo Shinshu" from my book, *Jodo Shinshu Buddhist Teachings*, Dharma Lion Publications, 2012, p. 176, or the revised version at http://amida-ji-retreat-temple-romania.blogspot.ro/p/three-refuges-in-jodo-shinshu.html . Also, read the article, *The Meaning of Arya Sangha in Jodo Shinshu* at, http://amida-ji-retreat-temple-romania.blogspot.ro/2015/12/the-meaning-of-arya-sangha-in-jodo.html

[23] Shakyamuni Buddha, *Samyutta Nikaya*, 3:25

Thus, we can die anytime, even when young. As Nagarjuna said:

"Life flickers in the flurries of a thousand ills,
More fragile than a bubble in a stream.
In sleep, each breath departs and is again drawn in;
How wondrous that we wake up living still!"[24]

Indeed, as unpredictable as life is in human form, we should consider it a miracle that we have reached the years we have now, and so we should strive more to understand Amida Dharma and receive faith.

A renowned Buddhist master gave the following good advice on how we should think on death in every circumstance of our life:

"Meditate single-mindedly on death, all the time and in every circumstance. While standing up, sitting or lying down, tell yourself: 'This is my last act in this world', and meditate on it with utter conviction. On your way to wherever you might be going, say to yourself: 'Maybe I will die there. There is no certainty that I will ever come back.' When you set out on a journey or pause to rest, ask yourself: 'Will I die here?' Wherever you are, you should wonder if this might be where you die. At night, when you lie down, ask yourself whether you might die in bed during the night or whether you can be sure that you are going to get up in the morning. When you rise, ask

---

[24] Bodhisattva Nagarjuna as quoted by Patrul Rinpoche in *The Words of My Perfect Teacher* (Boston: Shambhala, Revised edition, 1998), page 41

yourself whether you might die sometime during the day, and reflect that there is no certainty at all that you will be going to bed in the evening."[25]

If we reflect deeply as the above and become aware that we may die at any moment, we should never again postpone listening to Amida Dharma, ask questions to our teachers to solve our doubts and be sure we receive genuine faith in Amida Buddha.

Rennyo Shonin said:

*"Considering that the human realm is a place of uncertainty for young and old alike, we will surely undergo some sort of illness and die. Everyone must understand that, given the circumstances in a world like this, it is essential that faith be settled decisively and promptly - indeed, **as soon as possible** - and that we be assured of the birth to come in the Land of Utmost Bliss."*[26]

He also said:

"Because the impermanence of this world creates a condition of uncertainty for young and old alike, we should all immediately take to heart the most important

---

[25] Patrul Rinpoche, *The Words of My Perfect Teacher* (Boston: Shambhala, Revised edition, 1998), page 54.
[26] *Rennyo Shonin Ofumi: The Letters of Rennyo*, translated from the Japanese (Taisho, Volume 74, Number 2668) by Ann T. Rogers and Minor L. Rogers, Numata Center for Buddhist Translation and Research, Berkeley, California, 1996, p.102

matter, the afterlife, and, deeply entrusting ourselves to Amida Buddha, say the nembutsu."[27]

Awareness of death and impermanence is the best friend on the Buddhist path and a sign of wisdom, even if we cannot read a single letter:

"It has been said that those who do not know the importance of the afterlife are foolish, even though they may understand eighty thousand sutras and teachings; those who know about the afterlife are wise, even though they may be unlettered men and women."[28]

If we really understand death, knowing that it is always there, ready to strike at any time, causing us to lose our precious human birth, we will never lose time in Dharma matters.
Until receiving faith and entering the group of those assured of birth in the Pure Land, we should focus as much as possible on listening again and again the Dharma about Amida, ask question to clear our doubts and discuss about faith with members and teachers. Also, even after receiving faith, we should treat Dharma matters as being of primary importance, and continue to listen deeply to it for the rest of our lives. Knowing that death may come at any time, we should find assurance in

---

[27] *Idem*, p.118-119
[28] *Rennyo Shonin Ofumi: The Letters of Rennyo*, translated from the Japanese (Taisho, Volume 74, Number 2668) by Ann T. Rogers and Minor L. Rogers, Numata Center for Buddhist Translation and Research, Berkeley, California, 1996, p.107

the Nembutsu of faith, and long for what is really eternal and never dies - the Pure Land of Peace and Bliss:

"If you wish to attain faith and entrust yourselves to Amida, first realize that human life endures only as long as a dream or an illusion and that the afterlife in the Pure Land is indeed the blissful result in eternity, that human life means the enjoyment of only fifty to a hundred years, and that the afterlife is the matter of greatest importance."[29]

As we become aware of the impermanence of our bodies and the world arrouund us, we should understand deeply the impermanence of our so called "spiritual achievements".

This may be a truth which is hard to swallow, but Jodo Shinshu teaches us that our spiritual evolution is an illusion. What we think we obtained now, we can lose in the next moment. The ego cannot evolve; all it really does is to constantly adapt itself to various coarse or refined attachments. From material pleasures to spiritual satisfaction and false Nirvanas, the possibilities of deceit are endless to those who rely on personal power.

Looking at our life from the perspective of the impermanence of both our bodies and our so called "spiritual achievements", we can see things clearly and ask the right questions. **What will happen to me if I die today?** You should ask yourself this question - **what will happen to you if you die today?** Your so called virtues

---

[29] *Idem* p.23

are shallow, so your next birth, which may come even today or while you are reading these lines, is uncertain if you do not rely on Amida. This is the only thing that matters to you now. You are the man in front of the two rivers of water and fire[30], you are surrounded from all parts by all kinds of dangers which you cannot defeat by yourself, and Amida is calling on you. How can you not answer His call?

Especially, because you are an ordinary person, you can't afford not to be sure where you go after death. So, if you encountered Amida's helping hand, accept it immediately, without any second thought. You must not assume yourself any risk and do not allow death to catch you unprepared, that is, without faith (shinjin). Let smart guys and virtuous practitioners live in the so called "here and now", realize emptiness, oneness, or whatever they say they realize, but you stay humble and cling to the sleeves of Amida. **We, followers of Jodo Shinshu path, know we have no time to play with practices or concepts which are beyond our capacities and do not solve the problem of death and rebirth quickly.** We are not the kind of people who can afford any risk in such a matter.

Some people say that the nembutsu of faith is too much related with death and afterlife and that they prefer something (a practice or teaching) for the "here and

---

[30] Read the Parable of the Two Rivers and the White Path, by Master Shan-tao, and my explanations, here, http://amida-ji-retreat-temple-romania.blogspot.ro/2007/10/commentary-on-parable-of-two-rivers-and.html

now". The world of spiritual seekers is filled with such ideas of "here and now" being a supreme goal, that we must learn to live in the "here and now", and not think about death or after death. But this separation is only a delusion. In truth, death is not separated from the "here and now" as breath which comes out might not be followed by the breath which comes in. In the "here and now" we can lose everything; in the "here and now" we and our loved ones can stop breathing, in the "here and now" we may suddenly find ourselves in the afterlife, losing this human form, the chance of listening the Amida Dharma and receive faith.

Like in the good movie, "Groundhog day"[31], the minds of unenlightened people dwell constantly in an ever repeating "here and now". Unfortunately, they like this "here and now" so much that they even create spiritual ideologies to keep them focused on it. Being extremely attached to the "here and now", they refuse to speak about death and rebirth, or the aspiration to be born in Amida's Pure Land, calling it a reminiscent of folk religion or a distraction from the "here and now". Unfortunately, they will also die one day, in the exact moment they dream about ,"here and now" and will be born again, in another "here and now" - the same here and now, but painted differently. How sad this is…

I know that the Buddhas always live in the here and now, because they transcended life and death, as well as any limitations of time and space, but are those practitioners

---

[31] A movie in which the principal character repeats the same day over and over again.

whose mouths are filled with "here and now", really living in the here and now of the Buddhas? It is important to understand that **unenlightened beings never dwell in the "here and now", but only dream in the "here and now".** They move, they live, they die and are born again in the "here and now" dream and slavery of samsara. Without rebirth in the enlightened realm of Amida Buddha, ordinary beings cannot hope for true awakening.

Children should not behave like adults. Similarly, unenlightened beings should not imitate the speech and actions of Buddhas or Enlightened Masters of the past. Until we actually transcend birth and death and attain Buddhahood, we should not speak too much about "here and now" and forget death.

Again, I urge all my Dharma friends to realize that there is NO time for the so called spiritual evolution. All we have is this fragile moment, this short break before death and another uncertain rebirth. In this moment we either accept Amida's helping hand or refuse it and waste our human life so hard to obtain.

There's no time, no time! There's no time for your so called "spiritual evolution"!
All you really have is this fragile moment between life and the next uncertain rebirth, so please, don't rely on the "achievements" or "virtues" of your deluded ego!
As you cannot make a mirror by polishing a brick, you also cannot transform yourself into a Buddha!
Understanding the two types of impermanence, of your body and your so called "spiritual realisations", don't

*lose your time in vain, and entrust to Amida.
Only by being born in His Pure Land after death you can safely get out of samsara and be able to benefit all sentient beings.*

Karma - the law of cause and effect

"Not in the heaven, not in the middle of the ocean, not in the mountain caves: there is no place in this world were you can hide from the consequences of your deeds."[32]

I will divide this section in two: a) general teaching on karma and b) karma and the salvation offered by Amida Buddha

a) General teaching on karma

Karma is the law of cause and effect. The term "karma" comes from the Sanskrit word "karman" which means action - acting with thought, deed and word. There are three types of karma: 1) the karma of thought, 2) karma of speech and 3) karma of action or body. All that we think, speak or do will affect our personal history. What we are now is the result of what we thought, said or did in the past, in another lifetime or in the present life; and what we think, speak and do in the present will create us in the future. We are the result of our own karma. The Buddha said:

"The joys and sorrows of beings
All come from their actions,
The diversity of actions
Creates the diversity of beings
And impels their diverse wanderings.
Vast indeed is this net of actions!"[33]

---

[32] Shakyamuni Buddha, *Dharmapada*.

In the moment of death, our personal karma determines the form and the vehicle, that is, the body which the mind-stream will have in the next birth. Our desires need a vehicle to follow them and fulfill them in another life. The environment where we are now, and where we'll be born in another life or the form (body) we have and we'll have, depend on the karma:

In the *Sutra of Instructions to the King*, it is said:

*"When the moment comes to leave, O King,
Neither possesions, friends nor family can follow.
But wherever beings come from, wherever they go,
Their actions follow them like their own shadow".*[34]

The doctrine of karma teaches us that we are completely responsible of what we are and of what we'll become. Nobody besides us, be it a god, human or any other being, can be held responsible. We deserve what happens to us, even if it is hard to accept that:

"Beings are owners of karmas, heirs of karmas, they have karmas as their progenitor, karmas as their kin, karmas as their homing-place. It is karmas that differentiate beings according to inferiority and superiority".[35]

---

[33] *The Sutra of a Hundred Actions* as quoted in *The Words of My Perfect Teacher*, Patrul Rinpoche (Boston: Shambhala, Revised edition, 1998), page 118
[34] As quoted in *The Words of My Perfect Teacher*, Patrul Rinpoche (Boston: Shambhala, Revised edition, 1998), page 119
[35] Shakyamuni Buddha, *Majjhima Nikaya 135: The Shorter Exposition of Kamma*

Also, in the *Atthasalini* commentary, by Buddhagosha, it is said:

"Depending on the difference in karma, appears the differences in the birth of beings, high and low, base and exalted, happy and miserable. Depending on the difference in karma, appears the difference in the individual features of beings as beautiful and ugly, high-born or low born, well-built or deformed. Depending on the difference in karma, appears the difference in worldly conditions of beings, such as gain and loss, and disgrace, blame and praise, happiness and misery."[36]

By contemplating deeply the teaching on karma we come to understand birth, life and death in accordance with cause and effect. Everything that exists has a cause, and any cause will have an effect. In every second of our lives we reap the fruits of our thoughts, words and actions, and we plant new seeds by what we think, say or do. This is the true way of looking at what happens to us and the world arround. Trully, instead of "Mother Nature" we should say "Mother Karma". We are born and reborn from our karma, that is, our own actions. Even outside nature is a reflection of our collective karma. Our world, our plane of existence as well as all other planes of existence arise from karma[37].

---

[36] As quoted in *The Buddha and His Teachings* by Venerable Narada Maha Thera,
http://www.buddhism.org/Sutras/BuddhaTeachings/page_18.html#_edn9

[37] See the chapter, "Some Buddhist explanations on the origin and existence of the universe" from my book, *The True Teaching on*

Not only that the teaching on karma explains how things work in the world, why we are what we are, why we have this form (body), but it also assures us of our free will. We are what we think (karma of thinking), what we say (karma of speech) and what we do (karma of action or body) and we can always change this karma and thus create a more peaceful and pleasant way of life.

The karma can be positive, negative and neutral. Actions, thoughts and words that generate positive karma lead to our own happiness and the happiness of others. If the intention is to benefit others, and we act, speak and think accordingly, then we create positive karma. But if we are motivated by our minds poisons, we will automatically create negative karma:

"I declare, o monks, that volition (intention) is karma. Having willed one acts by body, speech, and thought." [38]

Actions, thoughts and words which are not motivated by harmfull or good intentions create neutral karma. However, because such a neutral karma does not have a positive effect on ourselves and others it is also considered non-virtuous, and so, the Buddhist disciples are encouraged to focus themselves on creating positive karma only.

There are many classifications of positive or negative actions in the Buddhist teachings, like for

---

Amida Buddha and His Pure Land, Dharma Lion Publications, Craiova, 2015, p.31
[38] Shakyamuni Buddha, *Anguttara Nikaya*

example, the ten transgressions and their reverse - the ten virtuous actions, the five gravest offenses[39], the ten kinds

---

[39] Shinran Shonin wrote about the five grave offenses in his *Kyogyoshinsho*:
"There are two traditions concerning the five grave offenses. One is the five grave offenses of the three vehicles: 1) intentionally killing one's father; 2) intentionally killing one's mother; 3) intentionally killing an arhat; 4) disrupting the harmony of the sangha through one's inverted views; and 5) maliciously causing blood to flow from the body of the Buddha.
These acts are termed grave offenses because they go against the field of benevolence and run athwart the field of merits. Those who give themselves to these grave offenses, when they deteriorate in body and die, unfailingly plunge into Avici ('uninterrupted') hell, where for one great kalpa they undergo pain without interruption; hence, these offenses are termed 'acts resulting in uninterrupted pain.'

The Abhidharmakosa lists five acts of uninterrupted pain similar to those above. A verse states:
Violating one's mother or a nun of the stage of nonlearning [equivalent to the karmic evil of killing one's mother]
Killing a bodhisattva who abides in meditation [equivalent to the karmic evil of killing one's father]
Or a sage of the stage of learning or nonlearning [equivalent to killing an arhat]
Destroying the cause of happiness in the sangha [equivalent to the karmic evil of disrupting the sangha],
And smashing stupas [equivalent to causing blood to flow from the body of the Buddha].

The second tradition is the five grave offenses of the Mahayana. The Sutra Taught to Nigranthas states:
1) Destroying stupas, burning sutra repositories, or plundering the belongings of the Three Treasures.

of karmic actions that cause sentient beings to attain shortened lives, etc. There are also various precepts to deter us from evil actions and encourage us to do what is good, like the five precepts for lay people, the ten main Bodhisattva precepts, the 227 precepts for monks and 311 for nuns, etc.

The ten transgressions are: 1) to destroy life, 2) to steal, 3) to practice sexual misconduct, 4) to lie, 5) to use harsh words and language, 6) to speak ill of others, 7) idle talk,

---

2) Speaking evil of the teaching of the three vehicles, saying they are not the sacred teachings, obstructing and censuring it, or attempting to hide and obscure it.
3) Beating those who have abandoned homelife, whether they observe precepts, have not received precepts, or break precepts; persecuting them, enumerating their faults, confining them, forcing them to return to lay life, putting them to menial labor, exacting taxes from them, or depriving them of life.
4) Killing one's father, harming one's mother, causing blood to flow from the body of the Buddha, disrupting the harmony of the sangha, or killing an arhat.
5) Speaking evil by saying there is no cause and effect and constantly performing the ten transgressions throughout the long night of ignorance.

The Ten Wheel Sutra states:
1) Killing a Pratyekabuddha out of evil intentions; this is destroying life.
2) Violating a nun who has attained arhatship; this is an act of lust.
3) Stealing or destroying what has been offered to the Three Treasures; this is taking what has not been given one.
4) Disrupting the harmony of the sangha with inverted views; this is speaking falsely."

8) greed, 9) anger, 10) to support and spread wrong views.

A fully negative action has four parts. For example, killing means to identify the being to be killed, having the intention to kill, commiting the act of killing, and the resulting death of the victim. If all these four parts are met, then we generate the complete negative karma of killing. The same applies to stealing, commiting sexual misconduct, lying, etc. If we only have the intention of killing someone, stealing, or practice sexual misconduct with him or her, and we contemplate that in our mind but don't carry on with the act, we still generate half of the negative karma associated with that specific offense by fulfilling the two parts out of the four above. Thus, our mind streams are already affected by contemplating and enjoying the possibility of doing various harmful actions or by being happy when we see others doing them. Mental problems of various kinds, or inner disorders, can thus appear as the effect of such distorted thinking. Just ask yourself, how many times did you wish the death of somebody, looked with greed and envy to his possesions, or desired his wife or her husband? Also how many times did you agree with and feel pleasure in your mind when you saw evil deeds done by others, or even argue in their support? Only by doing that in your mind you can be sure that you no longer possess the seeds of being born again in a human or higher realm. How much more if you actually fulfilled the above transgressions!

To kill is extremely evil because all beings identify themselves with their bodies, but to encourage others to kill, praise killing or being a cause for killing[40] is worse than that. If you do that you would cause not only your own downfall, but of others, too. Encouraging or promoting killing influences the minds of many who will further transmit the idea that killing is good, which might lead to many deaths and the creation of hell on earth.

Shakyamuni Buddha said:

"All tremble at violence;
Life is dear for all.
Seeing other as being like yourself,
Do not kill or cause others to kill."[41]

He also said:

"A disciple of the Buddha shall not himself kill, encourage others to kill, kill by expedient means, praise killing, rejoice at witnessing killing, or kill through incantations or deviant mantras. He must not create the causes, conditions, methods, or karma of killing, and shall not intentionaly kill any living creature[42].

---

[40] Like for example, to ask somebody to kill another being in your name.
[41] *Dhammapada*, 130
[42] The mind is the key factor in all Bodhisattva precepts. "Killing by expedient means": refers to the means employed to facilitate the killing of a sentient being, such as pointing out the whereabouts of a chiken to others, cornering it, binding its feet, forcing its head onto the butcher block, etc.

As a Buddha's disciple, he ought to nurture a mind of compassion and filial piety, always devising expedient means to rescue and protect all beings".[43]

The World Honored One mentioned in the *Suka Sutra* ten kinds of karmic actions that cause sentient beings to attain shortened lives and they are all related with killing:

"There are ten kinds of karmic actions that enable sentient beings to attain shortened lives as retribution: first, is to personally do the killing of beings; second, is to encourage others to enable killing; third, is to praise killing's method[s]; fourth, is to see killing and accordingly rejoice; fifth, is, from evil hatred thus, desire enabling of death and destruction; sixth, is, seeing the resented destroyed already, the mind giving rise to joy; seventh, is to harm others' fetus in the womb (abortion); eighth, is to teach others to destroy and harm; ninth, is to build and erect 'heavenly' temples, for slaughtering sentient beings as sacrificial 'offerings'; tenth, is to teach others to have war and fight, to injure and kill each other. These are the ten karmic actions that attain shortened lives as retribution."[44]

To eat meat, including the meat of animals that were not specifically killed for you - although it is a lesser transgression than killing - maintains the karma of killing

---

[43] *Mahayana Brahmajala Sutra (Bommo Kyo)*, also known as *Brahma Net Sutra*.
[44] *The Sūtra In Which The Buddha For The Elder Śuka Spoke Of Karmic Retribution's Differences (Suka Sutra),* passage translated at my request by Shen Shi'an http://thedailyenlightenment.com

because without a request or expectation from the public, there would be no one to kill beings and offer their flesh for sale. But even if we don't eat meat, the vegetables or the tea and cofee we drink were produced by killing many insects when planting, taking care of the plants and harvesting them, so one can hardly find any activity which does not involve in a smaller or larger way the harming of other beings. Simply stated, **there is no being arround us, in this world or in other worlds, to whom we can say that we have no karmic debts to pay**. Contemplating on that and the above, we can understand more deeply the urgency to escape samsara and attain Buddhahood for our sake and others.

To steal, which is defined as taking what was not given, is extremely grave too, because beings have great attachements to their possesions, and sometimes to take one's money or property might be the equivalent to killing him. Just imagine you would steal the entire monthly income of a poor mother who has three kids to feed. Those children can die from lack of medicine or food, and the mother can get ill and die too, because of grief. Just like killing, the effect of such an act can easily send one to rebirth in the lower realms.

Shakyamuni Buddha said:

"A disciple of the Buddha must not himself steal or encourage others to steal, steal by expedient means, steal by means of incantation or deviant mantras. He should not create the causes, conditions, methods, or karma of stealing. No valuables or possesions, even those

belonging to ghosts and spirits or thieves and robbers, be they as small as a needle or blade of grass, may be stolen. As a Buddha's disciple, he ought to have a mind of mercy, compassion, and filial piety – always helping people earn merits and achieve happiness."[45]

The sexual energy is extremely powerful, but if one does not keep it under control or does not sublimate it, then it will constitute an immense obstacle against liberation from samsara. There are many types of sexual misconduct mentioned in the sutras and treatises of various Masters, like for example, not being faithful to one's wife or husband, having sex with another's partner, with those who are under age, with non-humans, with someone of the same sex, with one's parents or blood relatives, a nun or a monk who took the precept of abstinence, to have sex in the wrong places (temples, outside of one's room), wrong time (during daytime), in the wrong orifices (anus or mouth) which are not made for sexual intercourse[46], sexual relations that are harmful, etc. Here are a few quotes on sexual misconduct and its consequences, from Shakyamuni Buddha:

"If one has sex at an inappropriate time or place, with someone who is not one's wife, or not a woman, one is guilty of sexual misconduct. [...]

---

[45] *Mahayana Brahmajala Sutra (Bommo Kyo)*, also known as *Brahma Net Sutra*.
[46] "What are inappropriate body parts? The mouth, the anus [...]". Asvagosha as quoted in *The Great Treatise on the Stages on the Path to Enlightenment*, by Tsong-kha-pa, Snow Lion Publications, Ithaca, New York, p. 220

If one has sex with oneself or someone by the road, beside a pagoda or temple, or in an assembly, one is guilty of sexual misconduct. If one has sex with someone who, though under the protection of the king, or parents or brothers, has kept a tryst or accepted one's invitation or payment, one is guilty of sexual misconduct. If one has sex beside a holy statue or painting, or a corpse, one is guilty of sexual misconduct. One is guilty of sexual misconduct if, while having sex with one's wife, one thinks of her as another woman; or if, while having sex with another's wife, one thinks of her as one's own wife. Sexual misconduct can be grave or minor. If it is driven by strong afflictions, it is grave; if it is driven by weak afflictions, it is minor."[47]

"Likewise, endless varieties of punishments in a future life are described for the wrong deed of sexual intercourse between two men.
The one who commits misconduct with boys sees boys being swept away in the Acid River who cry out to him, and owing to the suffering and pain born of his deep affection for them, plunges in after them."[48]

"Abandoning sensual misconduct, he abstains from sensual misconduct. He does not get sexually involved with those who are protected by their mothers, their

---

[47] *Sūtra of the Upāsaka Precepts (Upasakasila Sutra)*, fascicle 6, Chapter 24a
[48] *Saddharma-smrtyupasthana Sutra.* Shantideva also quoted that passage from the *Saddharma-smrtyupasthana Sutra* in his work *Śikṣāsamuccaya (Compendium of Training or Compendium of Precepts)*.

fathers, their brothers, their sisters, their relatives, or their Dharma; those with husbands, those who entail punishments, or even those crowned with flowers by another man."[49]

"A disciple of the Buddha must not engage in licentious acts or encourage others to do so. Indeed, he must not engage in improper sexual conduct with anyone.
A Buddha's disciple ought to have a mind of filial piety – rescuing all sentient beings and instructing them in the Dharma of purity and chastity. If instead, he lacks compassion and encourages others to engage in sexual relations promiscuously, including with animals and even their mothers, daughters, sisters, or other close relatives, he commits a Parajika (major) offense."[50]

No matter if some modern people disagree, the sutras, that is, Shakyamuni Buddha's own words, but also the words of many Buddhist masters like for example Genshin[51] (the 6th Patriarch of our school), are very clear

---

[49] "*Uposatha Sila: The Eight-Precept Observance*", compiled and written by Somdet Phra Buddhaghosacariya (Ñanavara Thera), translated from the Thai by Bhikkhu Kantasilo. Access to Insight (Legacy Edition), 17 December 2013, http://www.accesstoinsight.org/lib/authors/nanavara/uposatha.html .

[50] *Mahayana Brahmajala Sutra (Bommo Kyo)*, also known as *Brahma Net Sutra*.

[51] Describing the neighbouring hells, Master Genshin comes to the so called Place of Much Suffering where *"are doomed to suffer such men as are guilty of sodomy. Here the victim, seeing the man he lusted with, embraces him with a passion like a hot flame which completely consumes his body. After he has died he comes to life again and runs away in great terror but only to fall over a terrible*

on what it means to engage in sexual misconduct and the karmic results of such an act. As in all Dharma matters, what Buddha said weights more than the opinions of unenlightened beings of various times.

To lie, to use harsh words and language, to speak ill of others and engage in idle talk are the four non-virtuous karma of speech. Among lying, the worst is to lie about one's spiritual realisations, but any other lie creates delusion and distrust among family, friends and other people. By using harsh words one can hurt others almost like beating or killing them, while by speaking ill, friends, families and even sanghas can be separated or slandered. Also by engaging in idle talk one spends his energy in useless speech and gossip that wastes one's own and other's time.

Shakyamuni Buddha said:

"A disciple of the Buddha must not himself use false words and speech, or encourage others to lie, nor lie by expedient means. He should not involve himself in the causes, conditions, methods, or karma of lying, saying

---

precipice where he is devoured by crows with flaming beaks and by foxes with mouths of flames".
Genshin said he quoted that passage in his Ojoyoshu from *Mindfulness of the Right Dharma Sutra* (Saddharmasm tyupasthana Sutra in Skr, Shobonenjogyo in Jpn). See, *Ojoyoshu*, in The Transactions of the Asiatic Society of Japan, second series, volume VII, 1930, translated from Japanese by A.K. Reischauer, http://amida-ji-retreat-temple-romania.blogspot.ro/2014/03/genshins-ojoyoshu-free-english-edition.html

that he has seen what he he has not seen or vice-versa, or lying implicitly through physical or mental means."[52]

"A disciple of the Buddha shall not praise himself and speak ill of others, or encourage others to do so. He must not create the causes, conditions, methods, or karma of praising himself and disparaging others. As a disciple of the Buddha, he should be willing to stand in for all sentient beings and endure humiliation and slander – accepting blame and letting sentient beings have all the glory. If instead, he displays his own virtues and conceals the good points of others, thus causing them to suffer slander, he commits a Parajika (major) offense".[53]

To be greedy or stingy makes one's experience - even from this life - to some degree of the suffering of pretas (hungry ghosts) and is a cause for birth there after death. The greedy person lives only for himself and suffers from a mental hunger that is never satisfied. Shakyamuni said:

"A disciple of the Buddha must not be stingy or encourage others to be stingy. He should not create the causes, conditions, methods, or karma of stinginess. As a Bodhisattva, whenever a destitute person comes for help, he should give that person what he needs. If instead, out of anger and resentment[54]*, he denies all assistance –*

---

[52] *Mahayana Brahmajala Sutra (Bommo Kyo)*, also known as *Brahma Net Sutra*.
[53] *Idem.*
[54] The Buddhist disciple becomes angry and loses his temper because the other party keeps asking for help.

refusing to help with even a penny, a needle, a blade of grass, even a single sentence or verse or a phrase of Dharma, but instead scolds and abuses that person – he commits a Parajika (major) offense."[55]

It is also said that one moment of powerful anger destroys the good ones that have been accumulated over many years of serious practice. This can also lead to killing or hurting others, as no one knows what one can be capable of when one plunges in deep anger.

Shakyamuni Buddha said:

"A disciple of the Buddha shall not harbor anger or encourage others to be angry. He should not create the causes, conditions, methods, or karma of anger.
As a disciple of the Buddha, he ought to be compassionate and filial, helping all sentient beings develop the good roots of non-contention. If instead, he insults and abuses sentient beings, or even transformation beings [such as deitis and spirits], with harsh words, hitting them with his fists or feet, or attacking them with a knife or club – or harbors grudges even when the victim confesses his mistakes and humbly seeks forgiveness in a soft, conciliatory voice – the disciple commits a Parajika (major) offense."[56]

"Do not speak harshly to anyone. Those who are harshly spoken to might retaliate against you. Angry words hurt

---

[55] *Mahayana Brahmajala Sutra (Bommo Kyo)*, also known as *Brahma Net Sutra*.
[56] *Idem*

other's feelings, even blows may overtake you in return."[57]

To slander and abuse the Buddha Dharma is the most evil deed because by destroying the Dharma one does something worse than killing the bodies of beings - he actually takes away their chances of freedom from all births and deaths. To slander and destroy the Dharma is like killing all beings over and over again, ad infinitum. Shakyamuni Buddha said:

"A Buddha's disciple shall not himself speak ill of the Triple Jewel or encourage others to do so. He must not create the causes, conditions, methods or karma of slander. If a disciple hears but a single word of slander against the Buddha from externalists[58] *or evil beings, he experiences a pain similar to that of three hundred spears piercing his heart. How then could he possibly slander the Triple Jewel himself?*
Hence, if a disciple lacks faith and filial piety towards the Triple Jewel, and even assists evil persons or those of aberrant views to slander the Triple Jewel, he commits a Parajika (major) offense."[59]

Master T'an-luan said:

*"If one says, **'there is no Buddha'**, 'there is no Buddha Dharma', 'there is no Bodhisattva' and 'there is no*

---

[57] *Dhammapada, 133*
[58] "Externalists" are non-Buddhists.
[59] *Mahayana Brahmajala Sutra (Bommo Kyo)*, also known as *Brahma Net Sutra.*

Dharma for Bodhisattvas', such views held firmly in the mind by one's own reasoning or by listening to other's teaching, are called, 'abusing the right Dharma.'"

"He who has committed the transgression of abusing the right Dharma will not be able to attain birth in the Pure Land, even though he has not committed any other evils. For what reason? The Mahaprajnaparamita sutra says:

[...] Those who have abused the right Dharma will also fall into the Great Avici hell. When the period of one kalpa comes to an end, they will be sent to the Great Avici hell of another world. In this way, such evildoers will consecutively pass through a hundred thousand Great Avici hells.'

The Buddha thus did not mention the time of their release from the Avici hell. This is because the transgression of abusing the right Dharma is extremely grave.
Further, the right Dharma refers to the Buddha Dharma. Such ignorant persons have abused it; therefore, it does not stand to reason that they should seek birth in a Buddha-land, does it?"[60]

---

[60] Please read the chapters "The karmic consequence of denying the transcendent reality of Amida Buddha and His Pure Land" from my book, *The True Teaching on Amida Buddha and His Pure Land*, Dharma Lion Publications, Craiova, 2015, p.109, "The 'exclusion' in the 18th Vow" from *Jodo Shinshu Buddhist Teachings*, Dharma Lion Publications, Craiova, 2012, p.168, "Those who deny the existence of Amida don't have shinjin - some simple explanations" from the same book, p.186 and the article *The 'Western mind' Excuse for Slandering the Amida Dharma* at http://amida-ji-retreat-temple-

Each negative actions causes four types of karmic effects. These are: 1) the fully ripened effect, 2) the effect simmilar to the cause, 3) the conditioning effect and 4) the proliferating effect.

1) The fully ripened effect
To do any one of the above ten transgressions while motivated by hate and cruelty causes one to be born in the hells, to do any of them while motivated by desire, greed and attachement causes rebirth as a preta (hungry spirit) and while motivated by ignorance leads to rebirth in animal form. Also, virtuous actions stained by all the mind's poisons, with no particular poison predominating cause birth in the human realm, virtuous actions stained by jealousy and rivalry, by doing something good only to prove one's superior qualities are causes to be born in the asura (demigods) realm, and virtues stained by pride causes rebirth among the gods in the world of desire.

If we do any of the ten transgressions for a long and constant period of time, while motivated by a very strong intention, like extreme desire, anger or ignorance, we end up in hells. If the intention is not so strong and the period of doing any of the transgression is not long, then we are reborn as pretas, and if its not so strong but is done continually, for a long period of time, it causes rebirth in animal form.

2) The effect similar to the cause

---

romania.blogspot.ro/2016/01/the-western-mind-excuse-for-slandering.html

When those who were born in one of the lower realms, due to the fully ripened effect of their karma, are reborn again in human form, they experience the effects similar to the cause. Also, even in the lower realms there are various sufferings that come from particular causes.
The effects similar to the cause are of two kinds: actions similar to the cause and experience similar to the cause.

The first means the inclination to do actions that were the cause of the previous rebirth in one of the lower realms. For example, if we killed, we still have the inclination to kill, if we stole, we have the tendency to steal, if we practiced sexual misconduct, we continue to feel attracted to such a behavior, etc. This explains why even from early childhood some enjoy killing animals or insects, steal others belongings, or feel the urge to do any of the ten transgressions. Innate tendencies usually shows us what we used to do constantly in previous lives.

The experiences simmilar to the cause mean that because we did one or many of the ten transgressions in a previous life, we are now receiving some specific misfortunes related to them. For example, if we killed in a past life, the present life will be short or plagued by frequent or constant disease. Thus, some die as infants due to their karma of killing, while others live sickly lives until death.
If, in a previous life, we took what was not given, we now experience poverty or we suffer from robbery and various misfortunes which results in never having enough or losing what we gained with hard work.

If we practiced sexual misconduct we will experience unbalanced relationships with lots of fighting, arguing and various other difficulties.

If we lied, we are now lied by others, we are criticized, belittled, not taken seriously or falsely accused.

If we used harsh words and language we are now hit back with offensive and insulting words, and whatever we say will be a cause for problems in our lives.

If we spoke ill of others and sowed the seeds of discord we are now in difficulty to get along with friends, associates or people with whom we try to have various social or work relations. Also, our employees or people under our leadership do not get along well, do not listen to what they are told, are argumentative and recalcitrant, etc.

If we engaged in iddle talk, our words in this life will carry no weight and we will not be believed when we speak the truth. Also, we'll have difficulties when speaking in front of large crowds and we'll lack self-confidence.

If we were greedy and full of avarice in a past life we will continue to feel an unsatisfyed hunger for possesions and we'll meet various adverse circumstaces that will cause us trouble in fulfilling such desires.

If we were angry and wished harm on others we will live in fear and suffer various harm many times in our present lives.

If we supported wrong views in a past life, and after spending some time in the lower realms, we will continue to be influenced by false beliefs and we'll be easily deceived in spiritual matters or disturbed by various misconceptions.

3) The conditioning effect
Due to our former engagement in the ten transgressions, we appear in bad environments and places. For example, if we killed, we are born in places with mortal dangers. If we took what was not given, we are born in places affected by famine, where crops are destroyed by nature elements. If we engaged in sexual misconduct we are born in muddy, repulsive or squalor places. Lying causes rebirth in places where we experience mental panic and material insecurity. If we spoke ill of others and saw discord we will be born in places that are difficult to cross due to wild landscape. If we used harsh speech we are born in desolate places lacking vegetation and exposed to the elements. If we engaged in iddle talk we are born in infertile land with untimely and unpredictable seasons. If we were greedy we are born in inhospitable lands with poor harvests and various adverse circumstances related with such places. If we were angry and wished harm on others we are born in lands where we experience constant fear and many adverse conditions. If we supported wrong views we are born in bad places where we have no refuge and protectors.

4) The proliferating effect.
This reffers to the fact that whichever one of the ten transgressions, or evil act, we did before, we have the tendency to repeat it again and again. Thus, our evil deeds and the evil causes we plant tend to multiply and diversify, makig us drowning even more in samsara.

b) Karma and the salvation offered by Amida Buddha

The reason I insisted on the above explanations and passages in the section a) - general teaching on karma, is to help us realize the gravity of our daily thoughts, actions and deeds. If a honest person contemplates the above, he would naturaly feel overwhelmed by the realisation of his tendency to do evil. Indeed, how many times did we wish the death of somebody or even killed various beings (killing non-human beings like insects or animals is also an act that generates evil karma) or look with envy at what one has? How many times we got angry, use harsh language, practiced sexual misconduct, lied, or acted dominated by greed, etc? Perhaps some of us even spread wrong views that run contrary to the Dharma!

We must ask ourselves those questions and after realizing our incapacity to lead a life of constant virtuous actions, we should **immediately** take refuge in Amida Buddha, say His Name in faith and wish to be born in His Pure Land after death.

We must take refuge in Amida Buddha with the attitude of somebody who is about to die now, in this very moment, without having any more time left, nor the power to purify one's actions. Indeed, there is NO time for the so called, "spritual evolution", and the consequences of our evil karma will manifest without fail. If we already did some of the above ten transgressions (who haven't done any of them in this life or former lives and continue to do them?) it will be impossible for us, ordinary people, to purify them by our own power while we are still living our busy lives in this samsaric environment. We really have no guarantee that we can reach a moment in this life, which may end anytime, when we'll have no attachements, blind passions and delusions. The clock of impermanence is ticking, and the mind deposit of heavy karma is already filled to the brim.

     Apparently, by saying that sentient beings cannot free themselves from birth and death by their own power, it seems that Jodo Shinshu misinterprets or does not totally accept the doctrine of karma. However, Jodo Shinshu accepts fully the teaching of karma, just that it sheds light on a very important aspect that many usually tend to forget.
Yes, generally speaking, we can change our karma and thus decide to act in such and such a way, influencing our own destiny, but do we really always act as we wish? Suppose a person who drinks a lot since childhood and has now 40 years of alcoholism, can he give up alcohol just like that, by a simple act of will? Or someone who smokes since early childhood, can he really give up smoking over night? We see from experience that many smokers, alcoholics or drug abusers cannot give up their bad habits so easily, some of them even ending their lives without being able to stop their harmful behavior. How much more is the influence of the past habitual karma!

This habitual past karma is not what we did in a habitual manner in a single lifetime, but what we did and were concentrated on in many lifetimes. If it is hard to put an end to the habitual karma of smoking which lasts only for twenty or thirty years, how much harder or even impossible would be to stop the various bad karmic tendencies of many lifetimes! Also, as I explained at the proliferating effect of karma, we have the automatic tendency to repeat again and again the evil acts we did before, thus drowning even more in samsara.

So, **Jodo Shinshu doesn't deny free will in changing karma, but it insists on the truth that this will is so much weakened by the habitual karma of past lives that it becomes almost incapable of really changing something.**

When we have become accustomed for many eons and long kalpas with living in ignorance, hate, greed, jealousy, attachments, how could we not be influenced by this habitual evil karma also in this life and how could we end all these perpetual miseries just by force of will? We all know that a long time of drug abuse leads to dependency, a state in which the personal will of change is extremely limited and one needs immediate help from a specialist. **But we took the drugs of delusion for many lifetimes since the beginingless past!**

Jodo Shinshu teaching and method doesn't start by staring at the ideal: we all have Buddha-nature and we can become Buddhas, or at least do pure deeds and gain merits, but from the state of mind in which we dwell in the present moment. Thus, **entering the Jodo Shinshu path is like saying: "Hello, I am Josho Adrian and I am an alcoholic". The Jodo Shinshu Buddhist doesn't**

say: "Hello, I am Josho and I have Buddha-nature", but "Hello, my name is Josho and I am ignorant and full of blind passions, incapable of healing myself (attain Nirvana/Buddhahood)".

So, first in Jodo Shinshu we recognize our own incapacities and then we accept the medicine, which is the Primal Vow of Amida Buddha. We understand that we are so sick that we can no longer rely on ourselves and we agree to apply the only treatment that works in dependency cases like ourselves.

Someone who says, "I can become a Buddha in this lifetime because my true nature is Buddhahood itself" is someone who *"fails to understand the influence of good and evil karma of past lives"* and *"that every evil act done - even as slight as a particle on the tip of a strand of rabbit's fur or sheep's wool - has its cause in past karma."*, as Shinran said in the thirteenth chapter of *Tannisho*.

In the same way as someone who abused drugs for many years thinks that he can give up immediately his dependency, and after a few tries he ends up taking a super dose, also *"a person may not wish to harm anyone and yet end up killing a hundred or a thousand people"*. This is the heavy influence of karma from past lives. And this is exactly why we need Amida's salvation.

This salvation, as promised in His Primal Vow, doesn't depend on our own will, which is influenced by our good or bad karma from past lives, but it depends solely on Amida's Power of curing our illnesses and transforming us into Buddhas: *"it is by the inconceivable working of the Vow that we are saved"*.[61]

By contemplating on the teaching of karma and realizing our incapacity to always have pure thoughts, actions and words, we decide to turn our minds toward Amida Dharma and take advantage of the salvation Amida Buddha is offering to us, ordinary beings, who cannot escape birth and death by ourselves[62]. If we do that, the roots of our karma are cut, and although we continue to experience the results of past karma and to act as beings filled with illusions and blind passions until the moment of our death, our karma cannot plant further seeds into another life.

To explain how Amida's salvation works in the field of cause and effect, we must also understand the teaching on the transference of merit.

Usually, in the practices based on personal power the practitioner "earns" virtues or merits which he transfers

---

[61] Shinran Shonin, *Tannisho*.

[62] However, Amida Dharma is not an instrument to justify blind passions nor institutionalize them as normal behavior. Indeed, in its saving activity Amida Buddha makes no distinction between virtuous and non-virtuous people. But making no distinction, out of Great Compassion, between them, it does not mean that it supports or encourages evil. Please do not confuse being saved as you are with the idea that your actions are worthy and good. Instead of praising or justifying your blind passions, be ashamed of them and grateful to Amida's helping hand.

for his own Enlightenment. But in the case of Other Power (Pure Land) way, the transference of merits takes place from Amida Buddha to those who entrust to Him (His Primal Vow). This transference of merit (eko) carries the follower to the Pure Land where he attains Nirvana or perfect Enlightenment.
Shinran Shonin said in a hymn:

"When sentient beings of this evil world of the five defilements
Entrust themselves to the selected Primal Vow,
Virtues indescribable, inexplicable, and inconceivable
Fill those practicers".[63]

Shinran explained the merit transference from Amida to the practitioner as having two aspects:

1) the merit transference of going forth (Oso-Eko) and
2) the merit transference of returning to this world (Genso-Eko)

"When I humbly contemplate the true essence of the Pure Land Way, I realize that Amida's merit transference has two aspects: one is the aspect of going forth, and the other that of returning".[64]

---

[63] *The Collected Works of Shinran*, Shin Buddhism Translation Series, Jodo Shinshu Hongwanji-ha, Kyoto, 1997, p.406
[64] *Kyogyoshinsho – On Teaching, Practice, Faith, and Enlightenment*, translated by Hisao Inagaki, Numata Center for Buddhist Translation and Research, Kyoto, 2003, p. 5

The first refers to the fact that through Amida's transference of merit we go to His Pure Land where we become Buddhas, while the second one means that after we become Buddhas in the Pure Land by sharing the same Enlightenment as Amida, we return to the various samsaric realms and universes, to save all beings:

"Through the benefit of the directing of virtue for going forth,
We enter the directing of virtue for returning to this world.

Through great love, which is Amida's directing of virtue for our going forth,
We attain great compassion, which is Amida's directing of virtue for our return;
If not for the Buddha's directing of virtue,
How could we realize Enlightenment in the Pure Land?"[65]

Also 'merit transference' means that after we have been born in that land we awaken great compassion, with which we turn toward and enter the cycle of birth and death to teach and guide sentient beings. This is also called 'merit transference.'"[66]

---

[65] Shinran Shonin, *Hymns of the Dharma Ages (Shozomatsu Wasan)* in *The Collected Works of Shinran*, Shin Buddhism Translation Series, Jodo Shinshu Hongwanji-ha, Kyoto, 1997, p.411
[66] Shinran Shonin, *Kyogyoshinsho – On Teaching, Practice, Faith, and Enlightenment*, translated by Hisao Inagaki, Numata Center for Buddhist Translation and Research, Kyoto, 2003, p. 98

How do we receive the infinite and all powerful merits of Amida Buddha? By entrusting ourselves to Him, saying His Name in faith (Nembutsu) and wishing to be born in His Pure Land. These three items, faith, the Nembutsu of faith (the true Nembutsu is the expression of faith) and wish to be born in the Pure Land are what Amida Buddha asked us to do in His Primal Vow. Simply stated, He said that if we want to escape the endless cycle of samsara, we should have faith in Him, say His Name and aspire to be born in His Pure Land:

"If, when I attain Buddhahood, the sentient beings of the ten quarters, with sincere mind entrusting themselves, aspiring to be born in my land, and saying my Name perhaps even ten times, should not be born there, may I not attain the supreme Enlightenment".

Faith, nembutsu and wish (aspiration) to be born are all three aspects of faith, because if we trully have faith in Amida, then we automatically say His Name and wish to be born in His Enlightened Realm.

To better understand the merit transference from Amida Buddha to us, we can compare it with a blood transfusion, or an organ transplant. When a sick person receives healthy blood or a healthy vital organ he can continue to live, even if until then he was supposed to die. Thus, the blood or the organ he received becomes part of his own body and will function as if it has always been there.

In the same way, we who deserve to be born in the lower realms if we are left at the mercy of our unenlightened karma, by entrusting ourselves to Amida Buddha we receive His enlightened karmic merits which imbues our mind stream and leads us securely to His Pure Land. Even if we continue to have delusions and blind passions until we die and we are actually born in the Pure Land, we become united with Amida Buddha from this very life (we enter the stage of non-retrogression), as His own blood or enlightened karma circulates now through our veins.

It is impossible for us, ordinary people to enter the stage from which we do not retrogress from spiritual achievements, but if we rely on Amida, we are assured of escaping samsara at the end of our physical bodies.

Just imagine you want to reach by foot a certain place situated at a distance of thousands of kilometers away. You may think that if you are serious enough and you are persistent, you can reach the destination, but are you sure that you are capable of enduring the hardships of the road, the wild beasts, the winds, icy storms and tornadoes that will come in your way? What if you get sick and die before finishing the journey? If you rely on yourself, there will be no point in your journey when you could say for certain that you are assured of safely reaching the destination. Now imagine that somebody comes to you and offers himself to take you there on his plane. If you accept, you just enter the plane and you will be taken to the destination safely and in short time. The pilot is Amida Buddha, and the plane or vehicle is His Primal

Vow. Accepting to enter the plane is faith (shinjin) and the Nembutsu of faith. Being on such a safe plane, with such a good pilot, means that you are assured of reaching the destination, or in Dharma words, you are assured of birth in the Pure Land and of subsequent attainment of Buddhahood there.

Amida Buddha's salvation takes place within the law of cause of effect. Simply stated, He offers His help to you, and you have two choices, you either accept it, or refuse it. This helping hand of Amida and the fact that you accept it, is the cause, and the effect is that you are saved and brought to safety by it, which means that you are assured of birth in the Pure Land. Amida Buddha wishes to save us all, but He doesn't take us to His Pure Land by force, so if we do not wish to go there or we do not accept the existence of that enlightened realm or the existence of Amida as He was described in the *Larger Sutra,* then we'll not go there. Nobody can go to a place which he thinks it doesn't exist and can't be saved by someone whom he considers being an imaginary person.

Unlike this world in which we live now, the Pure Land is not the karmic result of our own actions and thoughts, but the manifestation of Amida's Perfect Enlightenment. We did not create that place, we do not control it, and we cannot go there through our own power. This is why we say Namo Amida Bu, which means "I entrust/I take refuge in Amida Buddha". By saying the Nembutsu of faith we are assured of birth in the Pure Land by the same Power and Buddha who created it.

Along the path of personal power, repentance is a very important method of destroying the negative karma. However, true repentance is not just a simple confession of mistakes, but a deep awareness which penetrates one's body and mind. Thus, Master Shan-tao explained that there are three types of genuine repentance:

"The high grade of repentance is to shed blood from the pores of one's body and also to shed blood from one's eyes.
The middle grade of repentance is to shed hot sweat from the pores of one's whole body and also to shed blood from one's eyes.
The low grade of repentance is to feel feverish all over the body and also to shed tears from one's eyes".[67]

Answering the question whether repentance is necessary in Pure Land Buddhism, Master Shan-tao says in the same book (*Liturgy for Birth*), that if the follower has faith in the salvation offered by Amida Buddha he reaches the same result as in the case of repentance:

"Even though one is unable to shed tears and blood, one will get the same result described above if one thoroughly attains the true faith (shinjin)".[68]

---

[67] Quoted by Shinran in his *Kyogyoshinsho – On Teaching, Practice, Faith, and Enlightenment*, translated by Hisao Inagaki, Numata Center for Buddhist Translation and Research, Kyoto, 2003, p. 247
[68] *Kyogyoshinsho – On Teaching, Practice, Faith, and Enlightenment*, translated by Hisao Inagaki, Numata Center for Buddhist Translation and Research, Kyoto, 2003, p. 247

Shinran also said in the *Hymns of the Pure Land Masters*:

"Persons who have thoroughly realized the true mind of shinjin (faith),
Because it is the diamondlike mind,
Are equal to those who accomplish
The three grades of repentance; thus Shan-tao teaches."[69]

and in *Notes on the Inscription of Sacred Scrolls*:

"To say Namo Amida Butsu is to repent all the karmic evil one has committed since the beginningless past."[70]

In chapter III of his *Kyogyoshinsho* Shinran presents a very important dialogue[71]. Somebody asked how can the evil karma of the five grave offenses and the ten transgressions, which would cause one to be born into the lower realms for many kalpas, is annihilated by the nembutsu of faith, thus making one to be reborn in the Pure Land? How this situation can be explained *"in the light of the law of karma according to which a heavier karma pulls one down? Furthermore, from the beginningless past, sentient beings have been given to acts of various defilements, and so they are tied to the three worlds. If, as you say, they can attain liberation from the three worlds by mere mindfulness of Amida*

---

[69] *The Collected Works of Shinran*, Shin Buddhism Translation Series, Jodo Shinshu Hongwanji-ha, Kyoto, 1997, p.380
[70] *Idem.* p.504
[71] This dialogue was taken by Shinran from *Commentary on Vasubandhu's Discourse on the Pure Land* by Master T'an-luan.

Buddha with ten repetitions of His Name, what will become of the bondage of karma?".[72]
The answer is wonderful:

"Suppose there is a room that has been dark for a thousand years. If a light is cast into the room even for only a short while, the room will instantly become bright. How could the darkness refuse to leave because it has been there for a thousand years?"[73]

Darkness may seem deep and strong when we live surrounded by it for many kalpas, but it disapears as if it never existed when it meets the Light of Amida Buddha. We can compare the various evils and blind passions among each other and say that some are heavier or darker than others, but with what can we compare the Enlightenment and Light of Amida Buddha?
Also, if we speak in terms of weak versus strong, some beings are more powerful than others, but who in this world is more powerful than a Buddha? Even the most superior gods who live for eons cannot compare themselves with a Buddha in wisdom, powers, purity and the capacity to save all beings.

In order to escape the black hole of samsaric existence, we need the infinitely powerful energy of Amida Buddha. Only that can pull us out from the repeated births and deaths.

---

[72] *Kyogyoshinsho – On Teaching, Practice, Faith, and Enlightenment*, translated by Hisao Inagaki, Numata Center for Buddhist Translation and Research, Kyoto, 2003, p. 162
[73] *Idem*, p. 162

We cannot build anything equally powerful through our own actions. **Our repentance is simply not enough to eliminate the evil karma of innumerable eons in which we piled mountain after mountain of greed, anger and ignorance.**

The karma which binds us to samsara is too strong for people like us, filled with delusion and blind passions, but for somebody who is already free from it, like Amida Buddha, nothing which belongs to samsara has any power over Him or the salvation He offers:

"The ten repetitions of the Name are stronger than the five grave offenses or the ten evil acts[74] and so this 'stronger' karma prevails, enabling the evildoer to escape from the three painful states of existence."[75]

Only a few repetitions of the Name of Amida Buddha, and even one saying which is done by relying on Amida Buddha's Power to save (the Nembutsu of faith), is able to destroy the roots of all our evil karma since the beginingless past. And is not just because **we** say it, **but because the Name we say is the Name of Amida Buddha in which He manifested all His enlightened karmic energy and virtues**:

"The ten repetitions of the Name arise from the unsurpassed faith by taking as object the Name of Amida

---

[74] The ten transgressions.
[75] *Kyogyoshinsho – On Teaching, Practice, Faith, and Enlightenment*, translated by Hisao Inagaki, Numata Center for Buddhist Translation and Research, Kyoto, 2003, p. 164

Tathagata of a glorious body of skillful means that comprises immeasurable merits that are true and pure".[76]

Thus, if one entrusts oneself to Amida Buddha and says His Name in faith, it is like putting a sumo wrestler on the same scale with a feather. Which one is heavier and pulls the other one down? Truly, the whole of samsara with all its worlds and universes, with the realms of various beings, from hell dwellers up to the most powerful gods, weights less than a feather in comparison with the Name of Amida Buddha.

By deeply understanding this, let our minds turn towards Amida's Primal Vow and be grateful for His undiscriminative Compassion:

*"If we had not encountered
Amida's directing of virtue for going forth and returning,
Our transmigration in birth-and-death would have no end;
What could we do then, sinking in this sea of pain? [...]*

*Casting off the pain of birth-and-death since the beginningless past,
We are certain of attaining supreme Nirvana.
This is through Amida's directing of virtue for going forth and returning;*

---

[76] *Idem*, p. 163

Our gratitude for the Buddha's benevolence is truly hard to fulfill".[77]

---

[77] Shinran Shonin, *Hymns of the Dharma Ages (Shozomatsu Wasan)* in *The Collected Works of Shinran*, Shin Buddhism Translation Series, Jodo Shinshu Hongwanji-ha, Kyoto, 1997, p.410

Samsara is suffering

As Shinran said in *Tannisho*, *"it is hard for us to abandon this old home of pain, where we have been transmigrating for innumerable kalpas down to the present"*. Our minds are conditioned by our habitual karma from begininglees time to think that we can find hapiness and fulfilement in the samsaric states of existence, and so we continue to project false images of beauty into various objects of desire and make ourselves dependent on them. However, if we look more deeply at samsaric existence with eyes influenced by the Buddha Dharma we come to realize that everything, from the worlds of the gods to the hell realms, is nothing but an ocean of suffering and insatisfaction. This awareness, as well as the previous three profound thoughts, will naturaly lead us to the only wish that worths something - to go out, to escape samsara and to attain the state of Buddhahood for us and all beings, including our dear ones.

In order to help us become aware of the painful reality of the samsaric existence and to make us desire to escape from it, Shakyamuni Buddha and all the Masters of our lineage and other lineages put great efforts in describing the six planes of existence:

"Leaving the unclean world means to abhor and to depart from this impure world. It means to depart not only from this human world but also from the entire six realms. These all taken together constitute what is called the Three Worlds.

There is no peace in the Three Realms. The Buddha explained them by comparing them with a burning house and by saying that it is like living in a house which is on fire. It is a thing above all others from which to separate oneself with a feeling of disgust".[78]

Thus, let us all carefully contemplate the various pains of samsaric existence until we are deeply impressed by them. Then, quickly turn our minds toward Amida Buddha, entrust our karmic destiny to Him and wish to be reborn in His Pure Land after death. As Master Genshin stated:

"Truly this world is a prison-house and the Pure Land is our true country. We should therefore make haste to dislike and escape from this prison-house and turn to our true country of the Pure Land".

As death comes to each one of us, we'll certainly die one day, due to the exhaustion of our karma which provided us with the present human life, and if we haven't yet entrusted ourselves to Amida Buddha, we'll be reborn in one of the samsaric realms impelled by the power of our karma. So please, contemplate the suffering inherent to all the six realms and try to imagine yourself there,

---

[78] *Ojoyoshu*, by Master Genshin, translated from Japanese by A.K. Reischauer and published in The Transactions of the Asiatic Society of Japan, second series, volume VII, 1930, http://amida-ji-retreat-temple-romania.blogspot.ro/2014/03/genshins-ojoyoshu-free-english-edition.html All quotes from Genshin in this chapter are from this edition.

because you"ll surely remain in samsara if you do not accept Amida's helping hand.

As slaves to their own delusions, blind passions and karma, unenlightened beings are reborn in a threefold manner:
1) in terms of the three planes of existence, they are reborn in the world of desire (kamadhatu), the world of form (rupadathu) and the world of non-form (arupuadathu);
2) in terms of the types of beings they are reborn as the six kinds of beings: hell dwellers (naraka), hungry ghosts (pretas), animals (tiryanc), humans (manusya), demi-gods (asuras) and gods (devas);
3) in terms of the type of birth, they are reborn in four ways, from the womb, like human beings, some animals and devas (gods) inhabiting the earth, from the egg, like birds and fishes, from heat and moisture, like some insects and worms, and by spontaneous birth, such as gods, pretas (hungry spirits) and hell-dwellers.

The world of desire (kamadhatu) is the lowest of the three planes of existence, and it contains (from the bottom to the top) the realm of hells, the realm of hungry ghosts, the realm of animals, the realm of humans, the realm of fighting spirits or demigods (asuras) and some realms of the gods. The world of form (rupadhatu) and the world of non-form (arupyadhatu) contain only the realms of superior gods. Now lets describe them in detail and contemplate the various sufferings and insatisfactions associated with each one of them.

1. Contemplating the suffering of hell beings

There are eight hot hells and eight cold hells. According to Shakyamuni, and various Buddhist masters who explained them, these eight hells have their own adjacent or neighboring hells (utsadas[79]):

"There are eight hells there that I have revealed, difficult to get out of, full of cruel beings, each having sixteen utsadas; they have four walls and four gates; they are as high as they are wide; they are encircled by walls of fire; their ceiling is fire; their sun is burning, sparkling fire; and they are filled with flames hundreds of yojanas high."[80]

Another type of hell are also
the temporary hells (pradesikanakara in Skt), which were created through the actions of one being, two beings, or many beings. As Vasubandhu explained, their variety is great and their place is not fixed, so they can be found in rivers, mountains, deserts, and elsewhere[81].

Before entering into any explanation of these hells I think it is very important to mention that all the tormentors, "hell wardens" or terrifying beasts who are sometimes described as applying punishment, are not living beings,

---

[79] According to Jeffrey Hopkins' Tibetan-Sanskrit-English Dictionary, the term "utsada" means "neighboring hell". Bodhisattva Vasubandhu also uses this term in his *Abhidharmakosabhasyam*.
[80] Bodhisattva Vasubandhu, *Abhidharmakossabhasyam*, English translation by Leo M. Pruden; Berkeley, Calif, Asian Humanities Press, 1991; vol 2, p 457.
[81] *Idem*, p 459

but manifestations of the evil karma of those born there. Thus, even if they are real for the the inhabitants of hell, they do not have an existence of their own. Vasubandhu clearly explained this in the 4th stanza of his *Vijnaptimatravimsaka*[82] and he stated the same in his *Abhidharmakosabhasyam*.

In my description of these hells I guide myself especially after *Yogacarabhumisastra (Yugaron)* of Asangha, *Abhidharmakosabhasyam (Kusharon)* of Vasubandhu and *Ojoyoshu*[83] by Master Genshin, who himself quoted the above mentioned Masters and works, as well as various sutras and treatises.

The Eight Hot Hells

1. Hell of Repetition or the Reviving Hell
The inhabitants of that hell see each other as mortal enemies and furiously fight with one another with huge and inconceivable weapons created by their karma, until everyone is cut into pieces. As Master Genshin said in the *Ojoyoshu*:

"Whetting their iron claws they proceed to scratch each other's eyes out and lacerate the flesh on each other's

---

[82] Edition translated in Muse'on, 1912, 53-90; the Tibetan, edited and translated by S. Levi, 1926

[83] *Genshin's Ojoyoshu – Collected Essays on Birth into the Pure Land*, translated from Japanese by A.K. Reischauer and published in "The Transactions of the Asiatic Society of Japan, second series, volume VII, 1930" Rearranged and republished for free distribution on http://amida-ji-retreat-temple-romania.blogspot.ro/2014/03/genshins-ojoyoshu-free-english-edition.html

thighs until the blood runs out and the bones are exposed. [...] they cut their flesh into slices with sharp swords as fish is sliced in the kitchen."

When they all lie dead, a voice from the sky of that hell says: "Revive!" and they immediately come back to life and restart their fight. The time they spend in that hell is described by Genshin as follows:

"One day and night in the realm of the four Deva Kings[84] is as long as fifty years of human life, and life in the realm of the Deva Kings lasts five hundred years. But one night and one day in this hell is equal in length to the length of life in the realm of the Deva Kings, and the victims have to remain in this hell five hundred years."

2. Hell of the Black Rope
The beings born in this hell, due to their evil karma, are seized by the hell wardens, laid down on the ground made of burning metal and marked with *"hot iron cords in both directions as a carpenter makes marks with his line"*. Then they are cut into pieces with burning saws and iron axes or disemboweled with swords along these lines. As soon as their bodies are thus cut into pieces, they immediately become whole once more and the process repeats itself over and over again.

Master Genshin also described another torment for those reborn in this hell:

---

[84] The realms of the various gods will be explained in the next pages, after all other type of beings are discussed.

"Sometimes they [the hell wardens] spread nets made of innumerable hot iron ropes and drive the sinners into these, and then an evil wind begins to blow which wraps the fiery nets around the sinners roasting the flesh and charring the bones. On the right hand and the left are high iron mountains. On the top of these mountains are fastened flagstaffs made of iron and an iron rope is fastened at either end to these staffs and thus stretches from one mountain top to the other. Beneath this rope are placed in a row a number of large caldrons filled with a boiling, steaming substance. The sinners, with heavy burdens fastened on their backs, are forced to walk across on this rope, and naturally they cannot help from falling into the boiling caldrons below. In these they are boiled for a long time till bones and flesh are reduced to an indistinguishable mass."

The time they spend in that hell is described by Genshin as follows:

"A hundred years of human life are equal in length to one day and night in the Toriten[85], and in this heaven life lasts a thousand years, but the length of life in the Heaven of the Thirty-Three gods is equivalent to only one day and night in this hell and here life lasts one thousand years. Those who have destroyed life or who have stolen anything fall into this hell."

3. Hell of Assembly or the Rounding-Up and Crushing Hell

Master Genshin described this hell as follows:

---

[85] Toriten is the Heaven of the Thirty-Three Gods.

"In this hell are numerous iron mountains arranged in pairs so as to face each other. There are in this place various ox-headed and horse-headed hell wardens who are armed with all sorts of pronged iron sticks and clubs which serve as instruments of torture. With these they drive the sinners before them and make them pass between the pairs of mountains, whereupon these mountains come together crushing the victims till the blood oozes out and covers the ground.

Then again there are iron mountains tumbling from the sky which crush the sinners into fragments like grains of sand. Sometimes the victims are placed upon a rock and crushed with another rock."

Other texts say that sometimes the mountains facing each other turn into the flaming heads of various animals which the hell-beings have killed in their past lives and who now throw themselves into one another, catching the poor people in the middle and crushing them to death. Again, like in the other hells, when the dwellers die, they are revived and the torture starts again as described above.

The time they spend in that hell is described by Genshin as follows:

"Two hundred years of human life are equal in length to one day and night in Yamaten[86] where life lasts two thousand years, but one day and night in this hell is as long as life in Yamaten and in this hell the victims must

---

[86] Yamaten is the Heaven of Good Time (Yama in Skt)

remain two thousand years. Murderers, thieves, and adulterers fall into this hell."

4. Hell of Lamentations
Here the beings are roasted in buildings of hot metal with no exit, or they are boiled and poured molten copper into their mouths which burns up their internal organs.
The time they spend in that hell is described by Genshin as follows:

"Four hundred years of human life are equal in length to one day and night in Tosotsuten[87], and in this heaven life continues for four thousand years; but the length of life in Tosotsuten is equivalent to only one night and day in this hell and here life lasts four thousand years. Murderers, thieves, adulterers and drunkards fall into this hell."

5. Hell of Great Lamentations
In this hell, the wardens put a multitude of victims into metal sheds with double walls blazing with fire and beat them with various weapons. The doors are all sealed and the beings there howl in pain thinking that even if they succeed in getting past the first door, they cannot get through the second. According to Genshin, *"murderers, thieves, adulterers, drunkards and those who use evil language fall into this hell."*

The time beings spend there is described as follows:

---

[87] Tosotsuten is the Heaven of Contentment (Tusita)

"Eight hundred years of human life are equal in length to one day and night in Kerakuten[88] where life lasts eight thousand years, but one day and night in this hell is as long as life in Kerakuten and here life continues for eight thousand years."

6. Hell of Scorching Heat

In this hell beings suffer by being cooked in huge iron cauldrons filled with molten bronze. Whenever they surface, they are grabbed by the hell wardens with metal hooks and beaten in the head with hammers until they lose consciousness. This loss of consciousness are their only moments of respite when they do not feel pain, but as it does not last long, the suffering is felt again and again.

Master Genshin described other terrifying scenes from the Hell of Scorching Heat:

"The hell wardens seize the sinners and make them lie on the ground, which is made of hot iron. Sometimes they make them lie facing upward and sometimes downward, all the time beating and punching them from head to foot until their flesh is beaten into a pulp. Sometimes they place them on a large roasting shelf made of iron and heated to an intense heat. Thus they roast them in a raging flame. Turning them over first on one side and then on the other, they roast them until they are burned thin. Sometimes they fasten them on a large iron skewer, sticking these through them from the bottom to the head,

---

[88] Kerakuten is the Heaven of Enjoyment of Pleasures Provided by Themselves (Nirmana-rati).

and scorch them thoroughly till the flames enter the vital organs, their joints and bones, eyes, noses and mouths. Then again they place them in a large cauldron and boil them like beans. And sometimes they place them on the upper floor of an iron house and cause raging flames of hot iron to envelop them from all directions, thus consuming even their bones and marrow".

To make us aware of the destructive power of the fire manifested in this hell, Master Genshin provided us with a comparison:

"If one should put a portion of this fire as small as the light of a firefly into this world of ours it would consume this world in a short moment. What must, then, be the suffering of these sinners whose bodies, tender like budding grass, are being burned in this hell! The victims in this place look longingly up at the fires in the preceding five hells, for these seem by comparison cool like snow or frost".

The time beings spend there is described as follows:

"Sixteen hundred years of human life are equal in length to one day and night in Takejizaiten[89] in which heaven life lasts sixteen thousand years, but the length of life in Takejizaiten is equivalent to only one day and night in this hell and here life continues for sixteen thousand years. Murderers, thieves, adulterers, drunkards, those who use vile language and heretics fall into this hell."

---

[89] Takejizaiten is the Heaven of Free Enjoyment of Manifestations by Others (Paranirmita-vasa-vartin).

7. Hell of the Great Scorching Heat
In this hell the beings are blocked inside blazing metal houses where hell wardens impale them through their heels and the anus with tridents of hot iron until the prongs push out through the shoulders and the top of the head. In the same time their bodies are wrapped in sheets of blazing metal.

According to Master Genshin, who himself quoted various sacred texts, the hell wardens, taking each sinner separately, torments him saying: *"Are you frightened as you hear the cries and see with your eyes? How much more then will you be terror-stricken when your body is burning like dry grass and tinder! However, the burning by fire here is not that of a literal fire but rather the hot passion of your evil karma. The burning of fire may be extinguished, but the burning of evil karma cannot be put out."*

This passage is extremely important because, as I repeatedly said, it shows that the fire of hell, the various places of terror which were described above and will be described in the following lines, as well as the hell wardens themselves, are manifestations of the sinners own karma. This is the reaping result of the suffering they inflicted on other beings. The various hells exist because of the evil karma of beings - it is the evil energy of their actions manifested in terrifying forms to torment them.

As Master Genshin said, *"the power of evil karma which the sinners have created for themselves suddenly hurls them into this raging flame"* of that hell. *"Among all winds the wind of karma is the strongest, and it is in this way that the wind of karma of men's evil deeds drags them to their doom."*

According to him, *"Murderers, thieves, adulterers, those who use vile language, heretics and those who degrade nuns who keep the precepts of purity"* fall into this Hell of Great Scorching Heat.

The time beings spend there is half of an intermediate kalpa, which is a period of time very hard to measure in human years.

8. Hell of Suffering without Interruption (Avici)
This hell is at the very bottom of the World of Desire and is the worst among all the hells. Nowhere in the world of desire or in any world can be found more suffering like here.

The fire in this place fills everything and there is no space left untouched. It is so violent that the bodies of the victims and the fire become indistinguishable. There is also not the slightest interval when the suffering of beings ceases. Their number is impossible to calculate, but although they hear the cries of pain made by other people, they cannot see them. All the torments of the previous hells are experienced here in more horrific ways.

After describing the various sufferings in this hell, Master Genshin said:

"The suffering in this hell is a thousand times greater than the combined sufferings of the preceding seven great hells and their separate places. The suffering in this hell is so severe that the victims envy the victims in the Hell of Great Scorching Heat, for the suffering in the latter seems to them like the pleasures in Takejizaiten. If the beings under the four heavens and the beings in the six Devalokas[90] of Kamadhatu[91] should smell the stench of this hell they would perish utterly. The reason is because all the victims of this hell are filled with putrefaction. [...] If a person should hear all about the sufferings in this hell he could not endure it and it would kill him. How terrible, then, it must be! Not one-thousandth of the horrors of this Avici hell has been told, for it cannot be described. No one could listen to the description, nor can it be compared with anything else. If anyone should describe it thoroughly or listen to a full description of it, he would vomit blood and die".

Bodhisattva Nagarjuna said:

*"Just as among all kinds of happiness
The cessation of craving is the king of happinesses,
So among all kinds of suffering
The suffering of the Avici Hell is most fierce.*

*The suffering of being viciously pierced
With three hundred lances for a full day
Cannot compare, cannot even be mentioned,*

---

[90] The six Devalokas are the six realms of the gods in the World of Desire.
[91] Kamadhatu is the World of Desire.

With the least sufferings of hell."[92]

People who committed the five gravest offenses, who slandered the right Dharma, denied the law of karma or the existence of Amida Buddha, made light of the Mahayana doctrine and made other grave karmic sins, are born in this hell. Life there is a whole intermediate kalpa.

Neighboring hells (ustada)

Yogacarabhumisastra (Yugaron) of Asangha and *Abhidharmakosabhasyam (Kusharon)*[93] of Vasubandhu, also describe the neighboring hells ("ustadas") which are attached to the previous eight great hells, at each of their four exits. Bodhisattva Vasubandhu said:

"What is the meaning of the word utsada? They are called utsadas because they are places of supplementary torment: in the hells the damned are tormented, but they are additionally so in the utsadas. [...] After having been shut up in the hells, the damned then fall into the utsadas."[94]

The trench of fire (Kukula):

---

[92] *Letter to a Friend*, by Nagarjuna as quoted in *The Great Treatise on the Stages of the Path to Enlightenment*, volume I, by Tsong-kha-pa, Snow Lion Publications, Ithaca, New York, p. 169.
[93] See *Abhidharmakosabhasyam*, English translation by Leo M. Pruden; Berkeley, Calif, Asian Humanities Press, 1991; vol 2, p 457-458
[94] *Idem*, p.458

When beings emerge from one of the eight hot hells, they see something which looks like a shady trench, but when they enter it, thinking that they finally found a place to hide, they discover that it contains a fire that reaches to their knees. This consumes their skin, flesh and blood when they put their feet in there, but reappears when they take it out.

The mire of excrements and putrescent corpses (Kunapa):
When they emerge from that trench, they see a river and urged by thirst they rush toward it, only to realize it is in fact, a mire of excrements and putrescent corpses of humans and animals, filled with all kinds of water beasts and worms with iron beaks which devour them.

The plane of razor blades (Ksuramarga):
When they emerge from that swamp they see green plain but when they arrive there, they realize that the grass is composed of sharp razor blades which pierce their feet to the bone. This also heals itself when they raise their feet, and is cut again when they step on the grass.

The forest of swords (Asipattravana):
When they escape from that place, they rush toward a beautiful forest, which when they get there it is revealed that the leaves of the trees are swords which grow on their metal branches. When the wind blows, those swords fall on those beings and cut them into little pieces, which are then devoured by the infernal Syamasabala dogs. When nothing remains of their bodies, they reappear and are cut again and again.

The hill with Salmali trees (Ayahsalmallvana):
Then the beings arrive at the foot of a hill with Salmali trees. At the top of this hill they see their former lovers, with whom they performed sexual misconduct, calling on them. Filled with the desire to be reunited with them, they start climbing, but the leaves of the trees point downwards and are piercing their flesh. When they reach the top, instead of their loved ones they are met by birds with iron beaks which tear out and eat their eyes. Then they see again their loved ones calling on them from the foot of the hill. Down they go and now the leaves turn upward, stabbing them in all places of the body. When finally they reach the object of their desire, it turns into hideous metallic women or men who embrace them and start eating them alive.

As Vasubandhu points in his *Abhidharmakosabhasyam*, the plane of razor blades, the forest of swords and the hill with Salmali trees constitute a single utsada or neighboring hell because they have in common punishment through injury.

The river of boiling water and burning ashes:
When the beings finally emerge from the hill with Salmali trees, they reach the river Vaitarani, of boiling water and burning ashes, which encircles the great hell. Master Vasubandhu describes their sufferings there:

"On both sides of the river there are persons armed with swords, lances and javelins, who push back the damned who would get out. Whether they plunge into the water or emerge, whether they go up or down the current, whether

they traverse in the two directions or are tossed about, the damned are boiled and cooked, as the grains of sesame or corn poured into a cauldron placed over the fire".[95]

In the *Mindfulness of the Right Dharma Sutra*[96], which was much used by Master Genshin, there is a somewhat different description of the neighboring hells. I will present them too, as they are quoted by Genshin in his *Ojoyoshu*. I mention that these are only a fragment of the hells described in that sutra.

Thus, among the neighboring hells of the Hell of Repetition or the Reviving Hell there are:

- The Place of Filth which is *"filled with hot dung and filth which is very bitter in taste and full of worms with hard bills. The sinners are put into this hell and forced to eat this hot dung while the worms crawl all over them, chewing and piercing their skin, gnawing their flesh and even sucking the marrow from their bones. Those who have killed deer or birds fall into this hell."*

- The Place of the Revolving Sword which is *"enclosed with black iron walls ten yodjanas in height. It is filled with burning fire, in comparison with which an ordinary*

---

[95] *Abhidharmakosabhasyam*, English translation by Leo M. Pruden; Berkeley, Calif, Asian Humanities Press, 1991; vol 2, p.458
[96] *Saddharmasm tyupasthana Sutra (Shobonenjogyo) – Mindfulness of the Right Dharma Sutra* was translated from Sanskrit to Chinese by Gautama Prajnaruci between 538 and 543. This sutra explains the causes of rebirth in the six states of existence. It was much used by Genshin in his *Ojoyoshu*.

fire seems like snow. When the body comes into contact with this in the slightest way it shrivels up as small as a mustard seed. In this fire hot iron sticks rain down in heavy showers. There is in this place also a forest of swords which are so sharp that a hair or even the sign of a hair coming in contact with them is cut into fine bits. How much more then is this the case with the bodies of sinners! Sometimes the swords fall down like a large waterfall from the sky. So great is the confusion of agonies here that no one can endure it. Those who have destroyed life with a covetous spirit fall into this hell."

- The Place of the Fiery Caldron where *"the sinners are put into an iron caldron and boiled like one boils beans. Those who have killed, cooked and eaten animals fall into this hell"*

- The Place of Much Suffering where there are *"innumerable trillions of pains. We cannot describe these in detail. Those who have bound people with fetters, beaten them with rods, compelled them to make long journeys, cast them down steep places, suffocated them with smoke, frightened children and, in short, all those who in any such ways have caused others to suffer, fall into this hell."*

- The Place of the Black Calm where *"the sinners are in pitch darkness and they are constantly being wasted with a dark fire. Then a raging storm begins to blow which forces Diamond Mountain to clash with the surrounding mountains so that the bodies of the sinners are crushed between them and the fragments are scattered like grains of sand. After this a hot wind blows which cuts like a sharp sword. Those who have killed sheep by suffocating them with fire and those who have killed turtles by crushing them between tiles fall into this hell."*

- The Place of No-Joy where there is *"a big fire which burns the bodies of sinners day and night. There are in it birds with red hot beaks, dogs and foxes whose cries are so blood-curdling that the hairs of the victims stand on end. They continually come and gnaw away at the bones and flesh of the victims which lie around in a confused mass. Worms with hard snouts pierce the bones and suck out the marrow. Those who have blown shells, beaten drums and made dreadful noises, or those who have killed birds and beasts fall into this hell."*

- The Place of the Most Severe Suffering which *"is located on the edge of a steep cliff where sinners are continually burning in a fire of iron. Those who have ruthlessly killed anything fall into this hell."*

Among the neighboring hells of the Hell of the Black Rope, there are:

- The Place of Crying-Receiving Pain where *"the sinners are placed on a precipice immeasurable yodjanas in height. They are tied together with black ropes of hot fire and when they have been thus lashed together they are pushed over the brink. As they fall they strike on the fiery ground below, which is studded with sharp swords as numerous as the blades of grass. Thereupon dogs with jaws of flaming iron chew them into fine bits, and though they cry out for help none are saved. Those who have been teachers of the Law but who have explained it with evil prejudices, thus failing to give the truth and indifferent to the consequences [...] fall into this hell".*

-. The Place of the Dreaded Eagle where *"the hell wardens, wielding their iron clubs with great wrath, strike the sinners suddenly and do violence to them day and night. Sometimes they brandish their flaming iron swords and slash the victims, or drawing iron fiery bows with arrows affixed they cruelly shoot them, all the time driving them forward. Those who with a covetous spirit, have bound or killed others in order to rob them of their possessions, fall into this hell."*

Among the neighboring hells of the Hell of Assembly or the Rounding-Up and Crushing Hell, there are:

- The Evil-Seeing Place where *"those who with violence have committed fornication with other men's children fall into this hell and receive its tortures. The sinners think they see their own children in hell tortured by the hell wardens who take iron sticks and iron gimlets and thrust these into their privates, or using iron hooks they thrust them in and pull them out of the vagina. The sinners seeing this suffering of their children are filled with longing and pity for them so great that they cannot endure the sight. But if one compares the suffering caused by seeing this with the suffering caused by being burned in the fire, it is not one-sixteenth as great. After being thus tortured by seeing their own children ill treated they receive the suffering in their own bodies. First the hell wardens stand the victims on their heads and boil them in a fluid of molten copper which runs in at the anus and through the internals, thus burning the vital organs and finally running out from the mouth and the nose. The above mentioned kinds of suffering, namely, the suffering in heart and the suffering in body, continue for immeasurable hundreds of thousands of years."*

- The Place of Much Suffering where *"are doomed to suffer such men as are guilty of sodomy. Here the victim, seeing the man he lusted with, embraces him with a passion like a hot flame which completely consumes his body. After he has died he comes to life again and runs away in great terror but only to fall over a terrible precipice where he is devoured by crows with flaming beaks and by foxes with mouths of flames".*

- The Place of Enduring Suffering where *"must suffer those who have stolen and violated other men's wives. The hell wardens seize the sinners and hang them with heads downward from the branches of trees. Beneath them is a raging flame which completely consumes their bodies. They come to life again and then are burned as before. When they cry out in agony the flames enter their bodies and consume the vital organs. This suffering continues for immeasurable hundreds of thousands of years. Further description of this is found in the scriptures".*

Among the neighboring hells of the Hell of Lamentation there are:

- The Hell of Fire and Worms where those who have sold alcohol diluted with water fall into this place and *"their bodies are afflicted with the four hundred and four diseases. The power of one of these diseases is such that in a single day and night it would destroy all the inhabitants of the Four Islands[97]. From the bodies of the victims come out worms which eat up the skin, flesh and marrow."*

- The Place called Cloud-Fire-Mist where *"those who have forced women to drink alcohol and then violated them bringing them to shame fall into this hell, and they are tortured with a flame which is twelve hundred feet deep. The hell wardens lay hold on them and force them to walk through this fire until they are consumed from head to foot. When they seem utterly destroyed the hell wardens call out: "Revive! Revive!" and they come to life again. Then they drive them through the fire again just as before, and thus without any intermission in their suffering this is kept up for immeasurable hundreds of thousands of years."*

Among the neighboring hells of the Hell of Great Lamentations there are:

- The Place called Receiving-Baring-Suffering where *"the sinners' mouths and tongues are nailed together with hot iron nails so that they cannot cry out"*.

- The Place called Receiving-Limitless-Suffering where *"the hell wardens cut out the victims' tongues with hot*

---

[97] Four islands means Japan with its four major islands.

iron shears. After they have been cut out they grow on again but only to be cut out again. They also pull out their eyes just as they do their tongues, and without any intermission they slash their bodies with knives. These knives are so sharp that they can cut even iron and stone. How easily, then, do they cut human flesh! Such various and innumerable sufferings are the lot of all those who have used evil language. There are many such teachings in the scriptures."

Among the neighboring hells of the Hell of Scorching Heat there are:

- The Place called Fundarikiya where *"the bodies of the sinners are roasted in a flame until there is not a spot as large as a mustard seed which is not burned.*
All the people in this hell keep saying to one another: "All ye, come quickly, come quickly! Here is
the Lake Fundarikiya. Here is water to drink. Here is the cool shade of a wood." Lured on by these words, the sinners rush forward, but on either side of the road are pits filled with fire into which they all fall and where they are consumed skin and bone. After a little while they come to life again and the terrible heat makes them long for the water and so they press on until they enter the place of Fundarikiya. Now the flames of Fundarikiya are five hundred yodjanas in height. When the victims have been burned to death in this flame they come to life again after a little while, and then this process is repeated as before. Into this hell fall all those who have starved themselves to death in the hope of thus earning their way

into heaven, also those who have taught this heresy to others".

- The Place called Dark-Fire-Wind where *"the sinners are carried up into the sky by an evil wind, and as they have nothing to which they can cling they are twirled around and around like the wheel of a cart so that they become invisible to the eye. And while they are being thus twirled around and around another wind arises which is sharp like a sword and which cuts them into pieces as small as grains of sand and then scatters the fragments in all directions. By and by the fragments come together again and the victims come to life once more but only to be cut up and scattered as before. This process goes on endlessly. In this way are punished all heretics who hold the view that all existence is divided into Things Permanent and Things Impermanent and the view that the Impermanent is the body and the Permanent, the Four Great Elements".*

Among the neighboring hells of the Hell of Great Scorching Heat there are:

- A place which is filled so completely with flames that *"there is not a spot as large as the eye of a needle where there is no flame. Those who have violated pure laywomen fall into this hell".*
- The place called Fully-Receiving-All-Suffering where *"the hell wardens, taking out their swords of flames, skin the victims from head to foot and then, without cutting the flesh, they place the raw skinned bodies on the hot iron ground and roast them. Then they*

pour over them molten iron. In this way they are tortured through immeasurable ten million thousand years. Those who have deceived nuns by giving them strong drink and destroyed their souls so that they have become immoral fall into this hell; also those who have corrupted women with riches".

Among the neighboring hells of the Hell of Suffering without Interruption there are:

- The place called Iron-Plane-Fox-Eating-Place. Here, *"over the bodies of the sinners in this place the flames of fire rage for a distance of ten yodjanas. Among all the hells the torments in this hell are the most severe. Iron tiles rain down upon the victims, crushing their bodies and pulverizing their bones. Foxes with flaming jaws continually come and devour them. In this way the victims are tormented without ceasing. Those who have set fire to pagodas and temple buildings, burned images of Buddha, burned the homes of priests and burned the bed-room furniture of priests, fall into this hell."*

- The place called Black-Vomit-Place where *"the victims are so hungry and thirsty as a result of the heat which burns their bodies that they devour their own flesh. When, however, they have apparently consumed themselves they come to life again and begin once more to devour themselves. There is in this place a black-bellied serpent which coils itself around the bodies of the sinners and then gradually devours them from the feet up. Then again the victims are placed in a hot flame and roasted, or they are thrown into a large cauldron and boiled. Their bones and flesh are melted like ice in the spring, and this mass, mingling with the fire, unites to make one huge, raging flame. In this way the victims must endure inconceivable tortures of one kind and another for millions of years. Those who have stolen anything offered to a Buddha and eaten it, fall into this hell".*

- The place called Rain-Mountain-Gathering- Place. This is *"an iron mountain one yodjana in height which falls on the victims pulverizing them like fine dust. After this they come to life again but only to be crushed a second time. There are here also eleven flames which completely enfold the victims and burn them.*

Sometimes the hell wardens take their swords and slash the bodies of the sinners all over and then pour molten lead into the wounds. Then again the sinners are afflicted with the four hundred and four ills, and in various ways they are tortured for immeasurable millions of years. Those who have stolen and eaten offerings made to a Pratyeka Buddha fall into this hell".

- The place called Embado where *"there is an evil bird called Emba. The size of this bird is that of an elephant. It has a bill like a sword and this sends forth a flame. Seizing the sinners it carries them with flapping wings high up into the sky and, after soaring about for a while, drops them so that they plunge down like huge boulders and with such violence that their bodies are broken into hundreds of thousands of bits. But the fragments assemble again and the victims come to life, only, however, to be seized a second time and carried up and dropped. Their feet are lacerated by sharp swords with which the road is studded as thickly as growing grass. Dogs with teeth of flames come and gnaw and then devour them. In such ways they are tortured without ceasing. Those who plotted against others and starved them to death fall into this hell. Further accounts may be found in the scriptures".*

The Eight Cold Hells

These hells are located on the same level as the Eight Hot Hells, but in comparison with them, where fire is dominant, here the karmic environment is composed of snow mountains and glaciers and the winds are ravaging blizzards. All the beings born there are naked and experience the following torments[98].

1. Hell of Blisters (Arbuda)
In this hell various ice blisters erupt on the body of the beings while they are submerged in extremely cold water or blasted by the wind.

2. Hell of Burst Blisters (Nirarbuda)
Here the blisters become open sores.

3. Hell of Clenched Teeth (Atata)
Here the teeth of the beings are tightly clenched due to extreme cold. Master Vasubandhu explains that "atata"

---

[98] Patrul Rinpoche, *The Words of My Perfect Teacher* (Boston: Shambhala, Revised edition, 1998), page 68.

indicate the noise that the damned make under the bite of the cold, thus the name of this hell[99].

4. Hell of Lamentation (Hahava)
In this hell the beings greatly lament while their tongues are paralyzed and find it difficult to breathe or scream. This hell too, has its name after the specific noise made by the tormented beings.

5. Hell of Groans (Huhuva)
Here the voices of beings are cracked and long groans escape from their lips. It is again a hell named after the sound of pain specific to those born there.

6. Hell of Utpala-like Cracks (Utpala) or the Blue Flower Hell
The skin of beings born there is blue and splits into four petals-like pieces.

7. Hell of Lotus-like Cracks (Padma) or the Lotus Flower Hell
Here the red raw flesh of beings becomes visible, and the cold makes it split into eight pieces, which makes it look like a lotus flower.

8. Hell of Great Lotus-like Cracks (Mahapadma) or the Great Lotus Hell
Here their flesh turns dark red and splits into sixteen, thirty-two and then into innumerable pieces, thus looking

---

[99] *AbhidharmakoSabhasyam*, English translation by Leo M. Pruden; Berkeley, Calif, Asian Humanities Press, 1991; vol 2, p. 459

like a large lotus flower. Worms penetrate the cracked flesh and devour it with their metal beaks.

According to the sacred texts the lifespan in the first cold hell lasts as long as it would take to empty an extremely large container filled with sesame seeds by removing a single grain every one hundred year. The lifetime and suffering in the following seven cold hells is progressively twenty times more.

The *Jatakamala*[100] describes that the beings in the cold hells dwell in darkness:

"In the future life of a nihilist
A cold wind will rise in that place of absolute darkness.
Since it will make you so ill that even your bones will be destroyed,
Who will want to enter there to help you?"

In his *Letter to a Disciple*, Master Chandragomin[101] said:

---

[100] *Jatakamala* - *'The Garland of Birth Stories'* by master Aryasura describes thirty four of Buddha Shakyamuni's previous lives. This passage from *Jatakamala* was quoted in *The Great Treatise on the Stages of the Path to Enlightenment*, volume I, by Tsong-kha-pa, Snow Lion Publications, Ithaca, New York, p. 167. Many Tibetan scholars identify master Aryasura with the master Ashvaghosha.

[101] Chandragomin (Skt. Candragomin) - a famous Indian master and scholar from the 7th century and a lay practitioner, who famously challenged Chandrakirti to a debate in Nalanda that lasted for many years. His writings include *Twenty Verses on the Bodhisattva Vow* and *Letter to a Disciple*.

"An incomparable wind pierces your bones;
Your body shakes and freezes; you bend over and shrivel.
Hundreds of blisters rise and pop.
Creatures born from them eat and claw you; fat, lymph, and
marrow ooze out.

Exhausted, teeth clenched, all hair standing on end,
You are tormented by wounds in your eyes, ears, and gullet.
Mind and body stupefied by pain,
You dwell in the cold hell and emit a pitiful wail."[102]

The Ephemeral Hells

The ephemeral hells adjoin the hot hells and cold hells, but they exist in other regions, too. Master Vasubandhu said:

"There are the pradesika (ephemeral) hells, created through the force of individual actions, the actions of one being, of two beings, of many beings. Their variety is great; their place is not determined: river, mountain, desert, and elsewhere"[103].

---

[102] This passage from Chandragomin's *Letter to a Disciple,* was quoted in *The Great Treatise on the Stages of the Path to Enlightenment*, volume I, by Tsong-kha-pa, Snow Lion Publications, Ithaca, New York, p. 167.

[103] *Abhidharmakosabhasyam*, English translation by Leo M. Pruden; Berkeley, Calif, Asian Humanities Press, 1991; vol 2, p. 459-460.

The suffering experienced in these ephemeral hells varies considerably in both time and place. Thus, beings condemned by their own evil karma to be reborn in them may be trapped inside a stone, encased in boulders, held on the bottom of various lakes, boiled in hot springs, frozen in ice and glaciers, burnt in fire, eaten alive by various worms and insects, etc. Some also suffer by identifying their bodies with objects that are constantly put to use, such as mortars, brooms, doors, mats, hearthstones, pillars, ropes, etc.

There are many sacred texts in which the causes for birth in these ephemeral hells are presented, like appropriating or exploiting the property of the sangha, requiring large amounts of money for teaching the Dharma or for blessings, sacrificing animals, stealing from the public funds, adultery, and so on.

*

Now, after reading and contemplating the above descriptions and explanations of the various hells, we should all ask ourselves individually, what if I will be born in these hell realms? How could I endure such a horror and pain!

Bodhisattva Nagarjuna said in *Letter to a Friend*:

"Sinners who hear of the boundless sufferings in the hells
Separated from them only until the mere termination of their
breathing -
And are not completely terrified,

Have hearts as hard as diamonds.

*If you are frightened merely by seeing paintings of hell,
By hearing of it, recalling it,
Reading about it, and by representations of it,
What need to mention experiencing the fierce actuality of it?"*[104]

Please take each one of the specific sufferings in the hells and think deeply on them. Wouldn't you better accept Amida's helping hand that is extended to you out of His infinite Compassion and escape those places of torment?

2. Contemplating the suffering of hungry ghosts (pretas)

The realms of the pretas are to be found in two places: one is bellow Jambudvipa (our realm of human beings[105]), which is their main place of existence and is ruled by King Yama, and the other is between the realm of humans and the realms of the gods. Master Vasubandhu explains:

"The king of the pretas is called Yama; his residence, which is the principal dwelling of the pretas, is located under Jambudvipa. The pretas that are found elsewhere

---

[104] *Letter to a Friend*, by Nagarjuna, as quoted in *The Great Treatise on the Stages of the Path to Enlightenment*, volume I, by Tsong-kha-pa, Snow Lion Publications, Ithaca, New York, p. 168.

[105] The realm of human beings does not mean only the humans living on this planet. The Buddha Dharma recognizes the existence of many parallel universes and worlds.

are the surplus of the pretas. The pretas differ much one from another; certain of them possess supernatural powers and enjoy a glory similar to that of the gods".[106]

There are two kinds of pretas: 1) pretas who live collectively, and 2) pretas who travel through space.

1) Pretas who live collectively
Among the pretas who live collectively, there are three types: a) pretas who suffer from external obscurations, b) pretas who suffer from internal obscurations and c) pretas who suffer from specific obscurations.

a) Pretas who suffer from external obscurations
These are the pretas who suffer from intense hunger and thirst or from unbearable heat and cold. Thus, whatever food or water they see in the distance, it proves to be nothing but a mirage, because when they come closer, they realize it vanished, dried up or that it is guarded by armed demons who beat them and chase them away. As Master Genshin described:

"At times they succeed in finding a stream of pure water but when they rush to it and try to scoop up the water in their hands, demons of great strength come along and beat them with iron clubs, or the water suddenly turns into flames and burns them or it ceases to flow and is dried up". [...]

---

[106] *AbhidharmakoSabhasyam*, English translation by Leo M. Pruden; Berkeley, Calif, Asian Humanities Press, 1991; vol 2, p. 460

There are hungry spirits called Eating-Water whose bodies are parched with thirst. They rush about in search for water but cannot find even a drop. Their long hair covers their faces so that they cannot see. They run along the river banks and if there are people crossing they lap up the water which may be left in their foot prints, and thus moistening their parched throats they manage to exist. Or when people make an offering of water to the spirits of their departed parents they give a little to these spirits and so they prolong their lives. If the spirits try to take some of this water themselves then the various demons whose function it is to guard the water beat them with sticks. Those who in this life mixed water with the sake they sold, or those who put in earth worms and leeches and so did not fulfill the good Law (Dharma), receive this reward".

Also, as Genshin said, *"there are still other hungry spirit called Fear-Hope who live on the offerings which people make to their departed parents. Beside this they have nothing on which to live. Those who in this life rob the poor of even the little they have acquired through great efforts, receive this reward. Then, again, there are hungry spirits who are born on the seashore where there is neither cool shade nor river water and where it is so hot that even their winter days are more than a thousand times hotter than summer days on earth. They subsist on obtaining only the morning dew. Though they live on the sea shore, the sea looks to their eyes like a dry place. Those who in this life have taken advantage of merchants who have been overtaken with illness on their journey and have beaten down their prices and so robbed them receive this reward".*

b) Pretas who suffer from internal obscurations
This kind of pretas have very small mouths, some no bigger than the eye of a needle, and a large sized stomach of hundreds of meters or even more. When they try to drink water, the heat of their breath evaporates it as soon as it goes down their throats. In the same way, no matter how much they eat, they cannot be satisfied due to the contradiction between their mouths and stomachs, but even if they somehow manage to eat a little, it will burst into flames during the night and burn their inside organs. Also movement is extremely hard and painful to them because of their grass-like limbs.

Bodhisattva Nagarjuna said in his *Letter to a Friend*[107]:

"Some, with bellies as huge in size as a mountain,
Connected to mouths, the mere eye of a needle,
Are tortured by hunger, not having the capacity
To eat even the tiniest lump of filth thrown away.

Some, with bodies just skin and bones, and naked,
Are like the withered trunk-tops of palmyra palm trees;
While some blaze flames from their mouths in the sphere of the night,

---

[107] *Letter to a Friend (bShes-pa'i springs-yig, Skt. Suhrllekha)* by Nagarjuna, translated by Alexander Berzin, 2006, http://www.berzinarchives.com/web/en/archives/sutra/level6_study_major_texts/suhrllekha_letter_friend_nagarjuna/letter_friend.html

Having to eat blazing sand as their food, poured into their mouths."

Master Genshin also described such type of pretas who suffer from internal obscurations:

"Then there are hungry spirits called Eating-and-Vomiting whose bodies are very broad and a half yodjana in height. Their stomach and chest feel heavy, and so they continually try to vomit, but as they cannot succeed in this they suffer in various ways. Those husbands who in this life ate the good food themselves and gave nothing to their wives and children, and such wives as ate all the good food themselves and gave nothing to their husbands, receive this reward.

Then, again, there are hungry spirits called Eating-Odour who have to live on the smell of the food which sick people offer along the rivers or in forests. Those who in this life allowed wife and children only to smell the good food which they themselves ate, receive this reward".

c) Pretas who suffer from specific obscurations
The experiences of this kind of pretas vary from one another, according to the specific causes that brought them into that state. For example, some have many creatures living on their bodies and devouring them, or may have their own food transformed into various uneatable and foul matters, while some other cut their own flesh and eat it.

As Master Genshin said, quoting
Nagarjuna's *Prajnaparamita-sastra*:

"Then there are hungry spirits who have nothing at all to eat, and so they break open their own skulls and eat their brains. Again, there are hungry spirits who emit flames from their mouths and live upon the moths which happen to fly into these flames. There are hungry spirits who feed on pus, phlegm and the remains of the washings of human dung."

Or as he described in his *Ojoyoshu*:

" There are other hungry spirits who for lack of food go to cemeteries and eat the cremated bodies, but this does not stay their hunger. Those who in this life were prison wardens and who ate the food intended for the prisoners receive this reward."

A specific obscuration is that which manifests upon the false teachers of the Dharma:

"There are hungry spirits called Eating-Law (Dharma) who run about on steep places where it is difficult to walk, seeking food but finding none. If they enter a temple and hear an exposition of the Law (Dharma) they obtain strength and manage to live. Those who in this life sought to obtain fame by a false interpretation of the Law receive this reward".

2. Pretas who travel through space

This category includes various types of pretas which are generaly tormented by constant fear and hallucination. Generaly speaking, they want to offload their pain on others, so wherever they go they do harm to others, thus many of them fall into hells when their life as a preta comes to an end. Even when they visit their dear ones from previous life, they bring only sickness, insanity and various other sufferings, which causes magicians and exorcists to harm and destroy them.
They also suffer from the distorted perceptions of other kind of pretas, like perceiving the sun of winter to be too cold, or the moon too hot in summer night. Their bodily form may be of various hideous animals, like ugly dogs, birds and others.

As we have seen, the causes of being born among pretas are various kinds of actions motivated by greed, avarice, jealousy, etc. Their lifespan is also described by Master Genshin as follows:

"One day in this realm is as long as one month of human life and existence here lasts for 500 [preta] years".

Other texts, including Nagarjuna's *Letter to a Friend*, say that the life of pretas can be even longer, like five thousand or ten thousand preta years.

Master Genshin said:

"The Shobonenjogyo[108] says that those who are cruel, covetous, jealous and envious fall into this realm of hungry ghosts (Spirits). By the cruel and the covetous are meant those who think only of their own things, who do not love others or give alms, and those who are never satisfied no matter how much they rob others".

In chapter four of his *Kyogyoshinsho*, Master Shinran quotes Master Che-kwan of Koryo[109]:

"Hungry ghosts are called pretas in Sanskrit. Their places of habitation are found in various realms. Hungry ghosts with much merit become spirits of mountains and forests or of graveyards. Those without merit dwell in filthy places, receive no food or drink, and are constantly whipped. Forced to dam up rivers and oceans, they suffer immeasurable pain. Those who harbor flattery and deception in their hearts and have committed the five grave offenses and the ten evil acts that belong to the lowest degree of karmic evil receive the recompense of this state of existence".[110]

*

At the end of this presentation on pretas, I would like to add another special category of hungry ghosts - **the powerful pretas who wish to dominate other beings through religion.**

---

[108] *Saddharmasm tyupasthana Sutra (Shobonenjogyo) – Mindfulness of the Right Dharma Sutra*.
[109] That passage appeared in *T'ien-t'ai's Discourse on the Fourfold Teachings*.
[110] *Kyogyoshinsho – On Teaching, Practice, Faith, and Enlightenment*, translated by Hisao Inagaki, Numata Center for Buddhist Translation and Research, Kyoto, 2003, p.334

As I explained above, there are various types of pretas, and not all of them are weak or tortured by mere hunger or thirst. Some pretas have great powers due to previous good karma and merits, as Vasubandhu said: *"the pretas differ much one from another; certain of them possess supernatural powers and enjoy a glory similar to that of the gods"*[111], but also great arrogance and pride.

Among the pretas, the category called gyalpos in Tibetan are the most powerful. "Gyalpo" means "king" or "royal" and it indicates the various leaders of the preta plane of existence, so they are from the same category Vasubandhu reffered to in the above passage. It is said that in their past lives they were great practitioners who accumulated merit, but were not able to overcome pride and arrogance, or they died with thoughts of hate, vengeance, etc.

Generally speaking, all the pretas have the tendency to influence others. They are all eager for attention, offerings, etc, but the gyalpos have the best power to put this wish into action. They can be masters of deceit[112], disguise in various ways, even take the appearance of great teachers of the past or Buddhas and Bodhisattvas, and they like to impart various so called "teachings". There are some stories of advanced Buddhist practitioners who were tricked by gyalpos. This category

---

[111] *AbhidharmakoSabhasyam*, English translation by Leo M. Pruden; Berkeley, Calif, Asian Humanities Press, 1991; vol 2, p. 460

[112] However, not all gyalpo spirits manifest a negative and imperialist attitude. There are also some gyalpo who can show interest in the Dharma, but as they have an inconstant character and pride and anger are some of their main features, they can be easily offended and manipulated by the Maras.

of pretas can also perform miracles and offer visions to make people entrust and obey to them.

Into my opinion, the abrahamic/monotheist religions (Judaism, Christianity, Islam) were caused by such powerful pretas with imperialist tendencies. All of these religions were founded arround visions, miracles and a central authoritarian "divine" figure who pretends total submission from his believers. The jealousy of the "god" of Old Testament is clearly expressed in the first of the ten comandments and in other passages of the same text. This is also accepted in Christianity:

"I am the Lord your God, who brought you out of the land of Egypt, out of the house of bondage. You shall have no other gods before me. You shall not make for yourself a graven image, or any likeness of anything that is in heaven above, or that is in the earth beneath, or that is in the water under the earth; you shall not bow down to them or serve them; for **I the Lord your God am a jealous God***, visiting the iniquity of the fathers upon the children to the third and the fourth generation of those who hate me, but showing steadfast love to thousands of those who love me and keep my commandments."*

Also in the Quran there are many passages like that, but I quote here only a few:

*"Follow what thou art taught by inspiration from thy Lord: there is no god but He: and turn aside from those who join gods with Allah."(*Qur'an 6:106)

"The worst of beasts in the sight of Allah are those who reject Him: They will not believe." (Qur'an 8:55)

"Muhammad is the messenger of Allah. And those with him are hard (ruthless) against the disbelievers and merciful among themselves" (Qur'an 48:29)

"I will cast terror into the hearts of those who disbelieved, so strike [them] upon the necks and strike from them every fingertip." (Qur'an 8:12)

"Fight those who believe not in Allah nor the Last Day, nor hold that forbidden which hath been forbidden by Allah and His Messenger, nor acknowledge the religion of Truth, (even if they are) of the People of the Book (Jews or Christians), until they pay the Jizya with willing submission, and feel themselves subdued." (Qur'an 9:29)

As we can clearly see here, such a "god" is clearly NOT an Enlightened being, but a person dominated by jealousy, frustration and anger, who shares his so called "love" only with those who love him or follow his instructions, and punishes the lack of obedience of fathers to the third and fourth generations. Also, in the case of the Quran, he encourages his worshippers to be ruthless with non-believers, whom he himself regards as "beasts" and does his best to terrorize them! Surely a being like that will sink even more in the lower realms, even in the hells, after his life as a gyalpo or powerful preta is over.

We can see clearly the difference between such angry spirits dominated by the need for attention and a Buddha who has undiscriminative Compassion for all beings, no matter they accept His teachings or not! A Buddha does not need the attention and worship of others[113], He is not affected if beings love Him or despise Him. Praise or critic do not influence Him. All He does for unenlightened beings arises from His pure Wisdom and Compassion:

"The Buddhas of the ten quarters think compassionately on sentient beings just as a mother thinks of her child."[114]

Also, how do all Buddhas try to convince us to entrust to Amida Buddha? Clearly, not by force, nor terror, and not by threatening to destroy us and our children to the third and fourth generations:

"Shakyamuni and all the other Buddhas
Are truly our compassionate father and mother.
With various compassionate means *they lead us to awaken*
Supreme shinjin (faith in Amida Buddha) that is true and real."[115]

---

[113] To worship the Buddha is karmically beneficial for the unenlightened beings, not for a Buddha, as He does not depend on anything.
[114] The 'Chapter of Mahasthamaprapta' of the *Sutra of the Samadhi of Heroic Advance*.
[115] Shinran Shonin, *Hymn of the Two Gateways of Entrance and Emergence, The Collected Works of Shinran, Shin Buddhism Translation Series*, Jodo Shinshu Hongwanji-ha, Kyoto, 1997, p.629

Surely, no good can come from entrusting to some worldly jealous and vengeful spirits, no matter if the teachings associated with them do contain some good elements, too. Powerful pretas (and their followers) can have their own spiritual evolution, some may be better than others, but certainly, not one of them is enlightened and none escaped from the slavery of the three poisons: ignorance, greed/attachement and aversion. Contrary to this, taking refuge in a Buddha will lead us, sooner or later, to Enlightenment. Thus, one must be extremely careful to whom he is entrusting oneself to, as the effect is simmilar to the cause. If we take refuge in samsaric spirits, no matter how powerful they are, we will never escape samsara; if we take refuge in the Buddhas, and especially in Amida Buddha, we will ourselves attain Buddhahood.

The monotheistic religions believe in the existence of a creator god. However, this runs contrary to the teaching of the Buddha, according to which unenlightened beings are the karmic cause for the existence of unenlightened samsaric realms. Their individual and collective karma actually manifested the realms, worlds and universes in which they live[116]. Contrary to this, Enlightened beings or Buddhas, naturaly and karmically manifest Pure Lands or Enlightened realms. If a so called "supreme being" created a world like ours that means he is not enlightened, because if he

---

[116] See the chapter "Some Buddhist explanations of the origin and existence of the universe" from my book, *The True Teaching on Amida Buddha and His Pure Land*, Dharma Lion Publications, Craiova, 2015, p. 31

was enlightened this world would have been perfect and inhabitted by perfectly enlightened beings. Amida Buddha (and any Buddha!) does not pretend to be the creator of this samsaric world, but only of His enlightened Pure Land, where He vowed to bring all samsaric beings for their final liberation (attainment of Buddhahood/Nirvana).

Any person who pretends to be the creator and owner of this world or any samsaric world is afflicted with arrogance and is hungry for power - a feature which is often found in some gods and especially in some powerful pretas (hungry spirits) who have connection with the human realms. The attitude of such spirits or gods is an imperialist one, that is, to receive the praise and submission of as many beings as possible. I often give the example of Baka Brahma, the god who was mislead by Mara into believing that he was *"the Omniscient, the Omnipotent, the Lord God, the Maker, the Creator, the Chief, the Ordainer, the Almighty, the Father of all that are and that will be"* and was corrected by Shakyamuni Buddha[117]. However, those who have such an imperialist tendency are not only from the realms of gods, but from the preta realms, too. My opinion is that most of the gods who live way beyond our human realm are more busy with enjoying their beautiful long lives, than dealing with the affairs of the humans. So, I think that the pretas are more connected with us, and more involved with our plane of existence. Knowing this

---

[117] See chapter "There is no supreme god or creator in the Buddha Dharma" from my book, *The True Teaching on Amida Buddha and His Pure Land*, Dharma Lion Publications, Craiova, 2015, p. 18

we must be aware of the category of powerful pretas who want to dominate others through religion, and do as Shinran advised us:

"Those who take refuge truly and wholeheartedly, freeing themselves from all delusional attachments and all concern with the propitious or unpropitious, must never take refuge in spirits or non-Buddhist teachings."[118]

3. Contemplating the suffering of animals

Bodhisattva Vasubandhu states:

"As for the animals, they have three places, the land, the water, and the air. Their principal place is the Great Ocean; the animals that are elsewhere are the surplus of the animals"[119].

Master Genshin also explains:

"The realm of animals is divided into two parts. The chief place is in the great sea, and branches are interspersed in the realms of humans and heavenly beings".

---

[118] Shinran quoted this passage in his *Kyogyoshinsho*, chapter VI, from the *Sutra of the Ten Wheels of Ksitigarbha*. *Kyogyoshinsho - The Collected Works of Shinran*, Shin Buddhism Translation Series, Jodo Shinshu Hongwanji-ha, Kyoto, 1997, p.273
[119] *Abhidharmakosabhasyam*, English translation by Leo M. Pruden; Berkeley, Calif, Asian Humanities Press, 1991; vol 2, p. 460

a) Animals living in the Great Ocean
In the Buddhist cosmology, the great ocean or sea is the immeasurable extent of salt water which surrounds the four continents inhabited by humans and the Mount Sumeru[120]. In that place there are many type of animals, some of which many times bigger than those living in our human continent of Jambudvipa. Some of them are born between the continents where there is no sunlight and where they cannot see even their own bodies. Their suffering comes mainly from eating each other, the bigger ones swallowing up the little ones, while they themselves are inhabited by tiny little creatures who feed on their flesh.

b) Animals living in different places
These are animals that live in some realms of the gods, in the human realms, and the nagas who live under the four continents or in the depths of water.
Nagas are similar to spirits but they are included in the category of animals because they have serpent-like form. Although they have some miraculous powers, they also suffer from various afflictions, which Master Genshin calls the three heats:

"Then there are the various kinds of dragons (nagas) which receive day and night and without intermission the tortures of the Three Heats".

---

[120] Mount Sumeru is a cosmological mountain, like an axis of the world. Every samsaric world or universe has a mount Sumeru, or an axis in relation with which all the six planes of existence are described.

These three heats which are sometimes named "the three torments" are: 1. their skin and flesh are burnt by a hot wind and sand-storm, 2. an evil wind strips them of their clothes and thus deprives them of any protection from the heat, and 3. they are attacked and eaten by Garudas, a kind of combination of spirit-like being with miraculous powers, in the form of a giant bird[121].

The animals who live in our realm and the realm of the gods suffer from both eating one another, and from exploitation. They are hunted or raised for their meat and various products of their bodies, thus experiencing inconceivable torments and almost none of them dying a natural death.

Bodhisattva Nagarjuna lamented the state of animals in the following verses:

"Even when in the state of an animal rebirth,
there are all sorts of sufferings:
Being slaughtered, tied up, being beaten, and so on.
For those who've had to give up [the ability for]
constructive behavior
leading to [a state of] peace,
There's the extremely unbearable devouring of one
another".

Some are killed for the sake of their pearls or wool,
Or bones, meat, or pelts;

---

[121] *A Dictionary of Japanese Buddhist Terms*, by Hisao Inagaki in collaboration with P.G. O'Neail, Nagata Bunshodo, Kyoto, 2003, p. 271 (Sannetsu).

*While others, being powerless, are forced into servitude,
Beaten with kicks, fists, or whips, or with hooks or with
prods."*[122]

The main aspects of animal realm is ignorance, fear and prevalence of instinct. Master Genshin described the cause of rebirth among the animals:

"This is the reward meted out to the ignorant and those who are without a sense of shame and who in vain receive the alms bestowed by men of faith but who do not repay such kindness."

In accordance with *Abhidharmakosabhasyam* by Vasubandhu, the lifespan of most long-lived animals is no more than an eon, while the life spans of short-lived animals is not fixed.

Concluding thoughts on the suffering of the lower realms

The hells, preta and animal realms are called the three lower realms, where suffering is more intense than in the rest of the six planes of existence. We must not only read about the various pain and suffering in the lower realms, but deeply contemplate on them until we become fully aware of their reality and that we too have a

---

[122] Verses 89 and 90 from Letter to a Friend (bShes-pa'i springs-yig, Skt. Suhrllekha) by Nagarjuna, translated by Alexander Berzin, 2006,
http://www.berzinarchives.com/web/en/archives/sutra/level6_study_major_texts/suhrllekha_letter_friend_nagarjuna/letter_friend.html

great chance to be reborn there. A master of the past once said:

"At present it is difficult to endure sitting for merely a single day with my hand stuck in burning coals, or to remain naked for that long in a cave of ice during the winter winds, or to go for a few days without food and drink, or for my body to be stung by a bee and the like. If even these are difficult to endure, how will I bear the sufferings of the hot hells, the cold hells, the hungry ghosts, or the animals devouring each other alive?"[123]

Another one also said:

"Examine whether or not you have previously created the conditions for being born in these miserable realms, whether or not you are currently creating them, whether or not you would consider creating them in the future. Since you will go there if you have created them, are creating them, or would consider creating them, think, 'If I am born there, what will I do then; will I be able to do anything?' With your head pounding, or like a man struggling in the desert, consider that there will be absolutely nothing you can do, and develop as much fear and dread as possible."[124]

---

[123] *The Great Treatise on the Stages of the Path to Enlightenment*, volume I, by Tsong-kha-pa, Snow Lion Publications, Ithaca, New York, p. 173

[124] Yeshe Bar as quoted in *The Great Treatise on the Stages of the Path to Enlightenment*, volume I, by Tsong-kha-pa, Snow Lion Publications, Ithaca, New York, p. 174

The more frightened we become when contemplating the three lower realms, the better it is, because that would make us really wish to escape samsara and take refuge in Amida Buddha, our Compassionate Protector:

"Saying, 'Who will protect me
From this great terror?'
I will stare, aghast,
And search all around for a refuge.

Seeing no refuge anywhere,
I will be completely dejected.
If there is no refuge there,
What will I do?
Thus, from today, I go for refuge
To the Conqueror, Protector of living beings,
The one who strives to rescue living beings,
The Mighty One who dispels all fear."[125]

If we do not contemplate on the sufferings of the lower realms, while we are still living in this human body, and take refuge in Amida Buddha to stop the causes of being reborn there, it would be extremely difficult to do that when we fall in the three lower realms where we do not have the capacities and conditions to hear or understand the Dharma. As Bodhisattva Nagarjuna advised:

"Reflect daily on the hells,
Both those extremely hot and cold.

---

[125] *Bodhisattva - caryavatara* by Shantideva, as quoted in in *The Great Treatise on the Stages of the Path to Enlightenment*, volume I, by Tsong-kha-pa, Snow Lion Publications, Ithaca, New York, p. 175

Reflect also on the hungry ghosts
Emaciated by hunger and thirst.
Observe and reflect on the animals
Overcome by the suffering of stupidity.

A human body in this world is difficult to obtain.
Once you have it, diligently stop
The causes of miserable rebirths".[126]

3. Contemplating the suffering of human realm

As I previously explained in the first section, life in human form is most desirable and does not contain the extreme pain of hells, pretas and animal realms. However, humans have their own difficulties and specific sufferings. Generaly speaking, these are called the Eight Sufferings, namely, birth, old age, disease, death, encountering what is unpleasant, separation from what is pleasant, not getting what one wants and the suffering associated with the five aggregates (skandas). Some of these appear in other realms of existence too, but here I will explain them in relation with the human realm.

1) The suffering of birth

According to the Buddha Dharma, life in human form starts at the moment of conception when the conscience of a being in the intermediate state (gandharva) enters the cell formed after the union of male

---

[126] Bodhisattva Nagarjuna as quoted in *The Great Treatise on the Stages of the Path to Enlightenment*, volume I, by Tsong-kha-pa, Snow Lion Publications, Ithaca, New York, p. 162

sperm with female egg (ovum). From that moment until birth, the new being experiences various kinds of sufferings associated with the different embryonic stages, which are described in some sutras, like for example, *Garbhavakrantisutra: The Sutra on Entry into the Womb*, and various treatises. Whatever the mother eats or drinks or if she passes through various painful or stressful situations can affect the unborn baby. Also, when the pregnancy reaches term, the baby (and mother too) experiences various sufferings associated with birth. Some can die at that moment, but even those who survive might go through suffering very simmilar with dying when they exit the womb.

Nobody ever came into this world smiling, but in a river of tears. Also, birth is the the first step to death, as everything which is born must die. We may have the impression of growth and maturing, but what we do in fact, is making another step toward death, another rebirth, another death, rebirth, death.... ad infinitum. The very fact that we were born is a sign that we have not escaped samsara yet, and if we do not use this precious human life well, our present birth will be just another cause for rebirth in the lower realms.

    2) The suffering of old age
    When becoming old our bodies deteriorates, the hair becomes white, wrinkles appear all over our face and forehead and we become unnatractive.
When becoming old physical strenght and vigor deteriorate and it becomes more and more difficult to sit or stand, walk, talk or do various activities.

When becoming old, our senses deteriorates too. Our eyes cannot see well and our ears cannot hear as they used to when we were young. We also lose memory and other mental faculties.

When becoming old we cannot enjoy our sense objects. We have difficulty in eating, drinking and cannot find happiness anymore in desirable objects.

Seeing how body and mind deteriorate as we approach death, ordinary beings which are attached to form cannot be happy.

Shakyamuni Buddha said in *Lalitavistara Sutra*:

"As aging progresses and we pass a certain point,
We are like a tree struck by lightning,
Withered by old age like a terrible, decrepit house.
O Sage, speak quickly about an escape from old age.
Age enfeebles the masses of men and women
As a windstorm strips vines from a grove of sal trees.
Age steals our vigor, skill, and strength-
It is as though we are stuck in mud.
Age makes attractive bodies unattractive.
Age steals our glory and our strength.
Age steals our happiness and subjects us to insults.
Age takes our vigor; age begets death."[127]

Jetsun Milarepa also said:

---

[127] *Lalitavistara* Sutra as quoted in *The Great Treatise on the Stages of the Path to Enlightenment*, volume I, by Tsong-kha-pa, Snow Lion Publications, Ithaca, New York, p. 276

"One, you stand yourself up as if pulling a peg from the ground;
Two, you creep along as though you were stalking a bird;
Three, you sit down like a sack being dropped.
When these three things come together, granny,
You're a sad old woman whose illusory body's wasting away.

One, from the outside your skin hangs in wrinkles;
Two, from the inside protrude bones where flesh and blood have
shrunk;
Three, in between you're stupid, deaf, blind and dazed.
When these three things come together, granny,
Your face frowns with ugly wrinkles.
One, your clothes are so ragged and heavy;
Two, your food and drink is insipid and cold;
Three, you sit on your mat propped up with skins on four sides.
When these three things come together, granny,
You're like a realized yogi being trampled by men and dogs."[128]

3) The suffering of disease
Disease, when it occures, changes our body's appearance, making it ugly.
Disease means lack of ecquilibrium in our internal elements and causes us to experience physical and mental pain.

---

[128] Jetsun Milarepa as quoted in *Words of My Perfect Teacher*, by Patrul Rinpoche, revised edition, Padmakara Translation Group, Shambhala, Boston, 1998, p.82

Disease makes us lose our desire for objects that we previously enjoyed, or if we still desire some things, we might not be allowed to enjoy them because it would delay our recovery or worsen our condition. Also our movement is limited and we cannot do the activities we like.

Disease can force us to take medicine, food or drink that we find repulsive and we might need to accept painful and violent therapies like surgical interventions, powerful drugs and so on.

Disease makes us lose our vital energy and if it is a terminal disease, it will cause tremendous pain to us and relatives. Indeed, who among ordinary people can accept a terminal ill with 100% serenity? More than that, some become frightened of death even when they are slightly ill, while others commit suicide because they cannot bear the pain or desperation after being left alone by their dear ones. People who are very sick cannot take care of themselves, so they constantly need to ask for the help of others which may come or not, or may last for a while until their friends or relatives are tired of taking care of them.

Usually, very few are capable of giving constant support in such times of crisis and the world's hospitals and asylums are filled with sick or old people abandoned by their dear ones.

Shakyamuni Buddha said in *Lalitavistara Sutra*:

"Hundreds of illnesses and the pain of rampant disease
Afflict us, just as humans oppress wild animals.
Regard the beings overwhelmed by old age and disease

And quickly speak about escape from suffering.

In deep winter, wind and great blizzards
Take the vigor from the grasses, shrubs, trees, and herbs.
In the same way, disease takes the vigor out of living beings;
It breaks down their faculties, physical appearance, and strength.

It will drain a great fortune in wealth and grain to the last.
Disease constantly humiliates living beings;
It harms them and is contemptuous of beauty.
It torments them, like the sun beating down from the sky". [129]

    4) The suffering of death
    Death is suffering because we are attached to our bodies and we identify with it.
Death is suffering because we are separated from relatives and friends.
Death is suffering because we are separated by the objects of our desires like our property, wealth and various possesions.
Death is suffering because when dying we might feel various pain in the body and mind.

Shakyamuni Buddha said in the *Lalitavistara Sutra*:

---

[129] *Lalitavistara Sutra* as quoted in in *The Great Treatise on the Stages of the Path to Enlightenment*, volume I, by Tsong-kha-pa, Snow Lion Publications, Ithaca, New York, p. 277

*"You die and pass on to another life, and in so doing
You are forever separated from people who are beautiful
and
beloved.
Like a leaf fallen from a tree, or the current of a river,
You will never return and meet them again.
Death makes the powerful weak.
Death takes you away, as a river carries away a log.
People go alone, unaccompanied, with no companion -
Powerless because their karma has its effects.*

*Death seizes myriad living beings,
As sea-monsters seize swarms of creatures,
As an eagle seizes a snake, or a lion an elephant,
As fire takes hold of grass, trees, and swarming
creatures."*[130]

He also said in the *Larger Sutra*:

"The reality of birth and death is such that the sorrow of parting is mutually felt by all generations. A father cries over the deaths of his children; children cry over the death of their father. Brothers, sisters, husbands, and wives mourn each other's deaths. According to the basic law of impermanence, whether death will occur in order of seniority or in the reverse order is unpredictable. All things must pass. Nothing stays forever. Few believe this,

---

[130] Passage from *Lalitavistara* Sutra as quoted in in *The Great Treatise on the Stages of the Path to Enlightenment*, volume I, by Tsong-kha-pa, Snow Lion Publications, Ithaca, New York, p. 277-278

even if someone teaches and exhorts them. And so the stream of birth and death continues everlastingly."[131]

As few become aware in due time of the reality of death and impermanence, most people do not strive to follow the Buddha Dharma, but on the contrary, do even more evil actions during their lives, and so, when death arrives, they experience various pains and fears. Hallucinations may occur even before their actual death, which are signs or their future rebirth in one of the lower realms. Also, when they finaly die, various apparitions of the intermediate state (bardo) manifest before their senses, but because they have no faith in Amida Buddha or in any Buddha, no one can protect them, and so, they are left at the mercy of their evil karma.

     5) The suffering of encountering what is unpleasant
     Unpleasant circumstances are of various types, causing us fear and pain. Meeting with enemies, we fear that we may be hurt, insulted, dominated, punished or even killed.
Meeting with unfavorable situations, we fear we may lose our wealth and possesions. Being caught up in rivalry of any kind, we fear others will be more succesful than us while we are left with nothing.

Bodhisattva Nagarjuna said:
"Amassing wealth, watching over it and making it grow will wear

---

[131] *The Larger Sutra on the Buddha of Infinite Life*, translated by Hisao Inagaki, Malaysia, 2012, p. 68

you out.
Understand that riches bring unending ruin and destruction".[132]

Jetsun Milarepa also said:

"In the beginning wealth makes you happy and envied;
But however much you have, it never seems enough.
In the middle miserliness tightens its knots around you:
You can't bear to spend it on offerings or charity.
Your wealth attracts enemies and negative forces,
And everything you've gathered gets used up by others.
In the end, wealth's a demon that puts your life in danger.
How frustrating to just look after wealth for your enemies!"[133]

6) The suffering of separation from what is pleasant

Such suffering occurs for example, when we are separated from a dear friend, partner or relative. We recall the good qualities of those we lost and we are filled with regret on what we should have said or done, but its to no avail as we cannot go back in time. Such is our attachement to our loved ones that we can even die or become ill when we are separated from them.

---

[132] Nagarjuna as quoted in in *Words of My Perfect Teacher*, by Patrul Rinpoche, revised edition, Padmakara Translation Group, Shambhala, Boston, 1998, p.86

[133] Jetsun Milarepa as quoted in *Words of My Perfect Teacher*, by Patrul Rinpoche, revised edition, Padmakara Translation Group, Shambhala, Boston, 1998, p.86

However, if we contemplate more deeply on our relations with parents, wives, husbands, children and friends, we might also come to realize some ugly truths about them. For example, although our parents cared for us and wished only our best, because themselves had illussions and were not aware of the urgent matter of liberation from birth and death, their actions did us many harm, too. For example, by focusing their education exclusively on how to achieve worldly success and fame, or if they advised us how to make money without taking into consideration any moral standard, they encouraged our greed and caused us to become even more trapped in samsara.
As Shakyamuni Buddha said,

"Later generations learn from previous ones to act likewise. Fathers, perpetuating their wrong views, pass them on to their children. Since parents and grandparents from the beginning did not do good deeds, were ignorant of the Way, committed foolish acts, and were benighted, insensitive, and callous, their descendants are now unable to realize the truth of birth and death and the law of karma. There is no one to tell them about this. Nobody seeks to know the cause of fortune and misfortune, happiness and misery, although these states result from such acts."[134]

Not to mention the cases when parents neglect their children or use them to satisfy their own selfish desires.

---

[134] *The Larger Sutra on the Buddha of Infinite Life*, translated by Hisao Inagaki, Malaysia, 2012, p. 67-68

Indeed, some human parents are no different than monsters who eat their own offsprings!

Also, there are children who were raised well by their parents, with great efforts and sacrifices, sometimes even by engaging in negative actions, but they turn against their mothers and fathers and hurt them in many ways. It is well known that many parents end up not in their own houses but in old age asylums. The sons or daughters justify this by saying its in the best interest of the parents, when the truth is they simply no longer wish to assume their filial responsabilities. By doing this, they treat their parents as things, not living beings who once cared for them and raised them in their own house, not in orphanages..... It is said in the sacred texts that one cannot repay his parents kindness even if he carries them all his life on his shoulders, so imagine what evil karma such unfilial sons and daughers generate for their next rebirths! Instead of being a support for their father and mother, worldly children act as obstacles toward the physical and spiritual health of their parents and make them realize they spent their lives in vain to raise them.

How true these words of Jetsun Milarepa sound for many parents:

"In the beginning, your son is a charming little god;
You love him so much that you cannot bear it.
In the middle he ferociously demands his due;
You give him everything, but he is never satisfied.
He brings home someone else's daughter,
Pushing his kindly parents out.

When his father calls him, he doesn't deign to answer.
When his mother calls, he doesn't even hear.
In the end, he is like a distant neighbour.
You destroy yourself nourishing a swindler like that.
How frustrating it is to beget your own enemies!
I've cast off this harness that tethers us to samsara.
I don't want any of these worldly sons.

In the beginning a daughter is a smiling little goddess,
Imperiously monopolizing all your best possessions.
In the middle, she endlessly asks her due:
She openly demands things from her father,
And steals them from her mother on the sly.
Never satisfied with what she's given,
She's a source of despair to her kindly parents.
In the end, she's a red-faced ogress:
At best, she's an asset to someone else,
At worst, she'll bring calamity upon you.
How frustrating she is, this ravaging monster!
I've cast off this incurable sorrow.
I don't want a daughter who'll lead me to ruin."[135]

Friends too can be deceiving, treatings us well when we are prosperous, and forgetting us when we pass through difficult times. Also, the love of friends can often transform itself into hate and adversity if big attachments and conflicting interests arise:

"In the beginning friends meet you joyfully, they smile

---

[135] Jetsun Milarepa as quoted in *Words of My Perfect Teacher*, by Patrul Rinpoche, revised edition, Padmakara Translation Group, Shambhala, Boston, 1998, p.88

And the whole valley rings with 'Come in!' and 'Sit down!'
In the middle they return your hospitality with meat and beer,
Item for item, exactly one for one.
In the end, they cause strife based on hate or attachment.
How frustrating they are, those evil friends with all their quarrels!
I've given up my dining companions of easy times.
I don't want any worldly friends."[136]

7) The suffering of not getting what one wants.

This type of suffering occurs when we put great efforts into achieving a worldly goal but we have no success. Frustration, disapointment and anger fill our mind streams and cause us pain. But even when we are succesful, what we have just gained will soon prove not to be enough, and so we continue our efforts to achieve more and more, thinking errouneously that one day we wil find complete satisfaction and not need anything. However, samsaric activities never end, and we come to neglect the Dharma in exchange for the delusional goals we ourselves, our family and society assigned to us. Parents, children, wives, husbands, the company we work for and others will always ask more and more from us and so, we will never find any real break in which to take care of what is really important - solving the problem of birth and death. Knowing this, Master Rennyo advised:

---

[136] Jetsun Milarep as quoted in *Words of My Perfect Teacher*, by Patrul Rinpoche, revised edition, Padmakara Translation Group, Shambhala, Boston, 1998, p.88

"Listen to the Buddha-Dharma by making time in your secular life. It is wrong to assume that you can listen to the Dharma when you have time"[137]

      8) The suffering associated with the five aggregates (skandas).
      All the physical and mental elements of a being are classified in five types of skandhas ("agregates"): 1) form (a generic name for all kinds of matter and the body), 2) feeling or sensation, 3) perception, 4) mental formations (mental states), 5) consciousness or mind.

For unenlightened beings all these five are causes of delusion and suffering. Our body organs may fall sick and create pain, we may experience hunger, thirst, too much heat or too much cold, etc. Also our feelings and sensations are the basis for attachment and aversion which is a cause for various pains. Perceptions are subjective experiences, and are the basis for disagreement and controversy, leading to conflict among people.
The non-virtuous states of mind
include ignorance, desire, anger, pride, envy, deceit, stinginess, laziness, forgetfulness doubt and harmful beliefs but also the drowsiness, agitation and distraction people may experience during practice. These too, are a a cause for suffering.

Reffering to consciousness or mind, in Buddhism we speak about the Eight Consciousnesses which are

---

[137] *Thus I Have Heard from Rennyo Shonin*, translated into English by Hisao Inagaki, Dharma Lion Publications, Craiova, 2008, p.82.

generated when our senses encounter their objects: 1) consciousness of sight, 2) consciousness of hearing, 3) consciousness of smell, 4) consciousness of taste, 5) consciousness of touch, 6) consciousness of mind, 7) impure (mind) consciousness, 8) the alaya (storehouse) consciousness.

The meaning of the first five consciousnesses is easy to comprehend, so I will not dwell upon them. The consciousness of mind integrates the perceptions of the five senses in concrete images and takes decisions concerning the exterior world.
The impure (mind) consciousness is the source of clinging and so the origin of the sense of ego as well as of the other illusions which are born from the fact that we take as real something which is merely apparent. This of course, leads to suffering.

The alaya consciousness or storehouse consciousness is the place where all the actions and experiences in this life and the previous lives generated by the seven consciousnesses are stored as karma, being the only consciousness which comes along with every birth. This consciousness influences at the same time the workings of the other seven consciousnesses.
We take this alaya consciousness with us in all our births in the various realms of existence. It contains the seeds of various types of karma, and it is the storehouse of the habitual evil karmic tendencies that we have cultivated for eons. Because of the karmic seeds contained in the alaya consciousness one may die a premature death, be stricken with unexpected disease or inexplicable

misfortune, overcome by strong desires, aversions and obsessions, can think and do things that one should never even imagine, etc. So strong is the influence of the alaya consciousness!

When Shinran is recorded as saying in chapter 13th of *Tannisho*: *"a person may not wish to harm anyone and yet end up killing a hundred or a thousand people"*, he is in fact referring to the influence of past karma contained in the alaya consciousness, but I already talked about this at the chapter dedicated to karma, so please return there if you wish.

*

In addition to the eight sufferings explained above we should also contemplate the following words of Bodhisattva Vasubandhu:

*"It is apparent that humans also have
All the sufferings of the miserable realms -
Tormented by pain, they are like hell-beings;
Deprived, they are like those in the Lord of Death's world [the
hungry ghosts].*

*Humans also have the suffering of animals
In that the powerful use force
To hurt and oppress the weak -
These sufferings are just like a river.*

Some suffer from poverty;

For others, suffering arises from discontent.
The suffering of yearning is unbearable.
All of them quarrel and can be killed."[138]

5) Contemplating the suffering of asuras (demi-gods)

As Master Genshin explained, the realm of Asuras is divided into two parts: 1. *"the creatures of this realm which are fundamentally superior live at the bottom of the great sea north of Mount Sumeru"*, and 2. *"the inferior creatures of this realm dwell among the rocks of the high mountains which lie between the four great continents"*.

Although they experience various pleasures and abundance which are far superior to those of humans and even rival those of the gods, they are constantly tormented by anger, jealousy, quarreling and fighting. Beings in the human realm who are more spiritually advanced than others, but who strongly manifest these characteristics will be born among the Asuras.
In their own realm, Asuras divide themselves in various groups and territories and fight never ending wars, while also, because they envy the pleasures of the lower realms of the gods, start useless conflicts with them, which they eventually lose.

---

[138] Vasubandhu's *Discourse of the Requisite Collections (Sambhara - parikatha)* as quoted in *The Great Treatise on the Stages of the Path to Enlightenment*, volume I, by Tsong-kha-pa, Snow Lion Publications, Ithaca, New York, p. 292

Bodhisattva Nagarjuna said:

"Also, the demigods, by their very nature, experience great
mental suffering
Because of their hatred of the splendor of the deities.
Though they are intelligent, they do not see the truth
Because of the mental obscurations characteristic of this realm
of rebirth."[139]

In some texts, the realm of Asuras is counted among the lower gods, because of the pleasures found there, or among the lower realms, together with hells, animals, and pretas, because of the pain they inflict to themselves.

In conclusion, life as an Asura is a pitiful one – filled as it is with joys and pleasures more than a human can imagine, but not being capable to enjoy it due to envy and conflicts.

6) Contemplating the suffering of the gods

The gods (devas) experience the most pleasure, health and comfort among all the beings of samsara. Also, the higher their plane of existence, the longer is their lifespan and the happiness they enjoy. However, they also meet with some specific types of suffering

---

[139] *Letter to a Friend*, as quoted in *The Great Treatise on the Stages of the Path to Enlightenment*, volume I, by Tsong-kha-pa, Snow Lion Publications, Ithaca, New York, p. 292-293

which I will explain after I describe in short, each deva realm.

In the World of Desire (Kamadhatu), there are six classes of gods with their specific realms.

The first realm is the Heaven of the Four Kings (Caturmaharaja), which are located on four cardinal points of the Mount Sumeru: 1) East: Dhrtarastra, 2) South: Virudhaka, 3) West: Virupaksa, 4) North: Vaisravana. Each of these divine rulers has their own following of Caturmaharajakayika gods.
As Master Genshin explained, *"one day and night in the realm of the Four Kings is as long as fifty years of human life, and life in the realm of the Four Kings lasts five hundred years"*.

The second realm is the Heaven of the Thirty-three Gods (Trayastrimsa) which is placed on the summit of Mount Sumeru. The most important god of this realm is Sakra (or Indra in some texts).
As Master Genshin explained, *"a hundred years of human life are equal in length to one day and night in the Heaven of the Thirty-three, and in this heaven life lasts a thousand years"*.

The third realm is the Heaven of Good Time (Yama or Suyama).
As Master Genshin explained, *"two hundred years of human life are equal in length to one day and night in Heaven of Yama, where life lasts two thousand years"*.

The fourth realm is the Heaven of Contentment (Tusita). Queen Maya, the mother of Shakyamuni Buddha was reborn there when she died, seven days after giving birth to Him. During His earthly life, Shakyamuni often made visits to this realm (and other heavenly realms, too) in order to teach the Dharma to His mother and the gods living there.
As Master Genshin explained, *"four hundred years of human life are equal in length to one day and night in Tusita, and in this heaven life continues for four thousand years"*.

The fifth realm is the Heaven of Enjoyment of Pleasures Provided by Themselves (Nirmanarati).
As Master Genshin explained, *"eight hundred years of human life are equal in length to one day and night in Nirmanarati, where life lasts eight thousand years"*.

The sixth realm is the Heaven of Free Enjoyment of Manifestations by Others (Paranirmitavasavartin). This realm is inhabited by Maras, which are celestial demons that usually go to the other worlds to obstruct practitioners from advancing on the Buddhist path. So, "Mara" in Sankrit language means "evil one", "adversary" or "tempter".
Their karma accumulated in past lives was good enough to make them reborn in this high heaven, but still, their lust for power and selfishness not being eradicated, transformed them into living obstacles for other beings. Thus, they do everything in their power so that nobody gets higher than their plane of existence.

The *Nirvana Sutra* lists four types of demons: 1) greed, anger and delusion; 2) the five skandas, or obstructions caused by physical and mental functions; 3) death; and 4) the demon of the Heaven of Free Enjoyment of Manifestations by Others (Paranirmitavasavartin). So, in the Buddhist texts the word "demon" is sometimes used with the meaning of internal demons, or personal blind passions and illusions, but also in the sense of an actually existing being or beings who disturb others from reaching freedom from birth and death. Nowadays, there is a common mistake among many so called "modern" Buddhists, who promote the idea that maras are only internal and not external demons, too. Please do not share their misunderstandings and single-heartedly entrust to Amida Buddha, which is the best way to be protected against the influence of such evil and powerful beings.

As Master Genshin explained, *"sixteen hundred years of human life are equal in length to one day and night in Paranirmitavasavartin heaven, in which life lasts sixteen thousand years"*.

Master Vasubandhu explained some of the features of the gods inhabiting these heavenly realms:

"The Caturmaharajakayikas, Trayastrimsas, Yamas, Tusitas, Nirmanaratis and Paranirmitavasavartins are the gods of Kamadhatu (world of desire). [...]
A small god or goddess appears on the knees, or from out of the knees of a god or goddess; this small god or goddess is their son or daughter: all the gods are apparitional. Among these gods, their newborn are

similar to infants of five to ten years. From five to ten years according to the category of the gods. Young gods grow up quickly. "[140]

To be "apparitional" means that newborn gods appear spontaneously, and not from a womb, like humans. At their birth they are similar to infants *"from five to ten years according to the category of the gods"*. These *"young gods grow up quickly"*[141], said Vasubandhu. Then he explained further:

*"In Kamadhatu,
1. There are beings whose objects of desire are placed (by outside factors) at their disposition; but they are able to dispose of these objects. These are humans and certain gods - namely the first four classes of gods.
2. There are beings whose objects of desire are created by themselves; and they dispose of these objects which they create. These are the Nirmanaratis.
3. There are beings whose objects of desire are created by others but who themselves dispose of these objects created by others. These are the Paranirmitavasavartins. The first enjoy the objects of desire which are presented to them; the second enjoy objects of desire which they create at their will; and the third enjoy objects of desire that they create or have others create at their will. These*

---

[140] *Abhidharmakosabhasyam*, English translation by Leo M. Pruden; Berkeley, Calif, Asian Humanities Press, 1991; vol 2, p. 465-466.
[141] The gods of the next sphere – the World of Form (Rupadhatu) are complete in their development from birth and are also born fully clothed.

are the three arisings of the objects of desire (kamopapattis)."

According to Nagarjuna's explanation from *Maha-prajna-paramita-sastra*:

"If the practitioner has not been able to cut through lust, he will be reborn among the six classes of gods of the desire realm [kamadhatu] where the five objects of enjoyment are excellent, subtle and pure. If he has been able to cut through lust (raga), he will be reborn among the gods of the two higher realms [rupadhatu and arupyadhatu]."[142]

This means that the one who is reborn among the gods of the World of Desire cut many other passions from his heart, but still remained with various forms of lust, while those who destroyed lust but still have other more subtle delusions, go to the next heavenly realms in the World of Form (Rupadhatu) or World of Non-form (Arupyadhatu).

The world of form is the effect of great meritorious deeds and strong meditation practice, while the world of non-form, where beings do not posses bodies of form, is the effect of high levels of samadhi (meditative concentration).

The gods of the Rupadhatu (World of Form) and Arupyadhatu (World of Non-Form) have an extremely long life in comparison with humans and gods of Kamadhatu (World of Desire), while also lacking the

---

[142] *Maha-prajna-paramita-sastra*, Lamotte, volume 3, p. 1162.

negative emotions from there. However, they still experience ignorance and delusion because they have not yet eliminated the belief in the false ego. By not eliminating the belief in the false ego their suppression of negative emotions is only temporary because such a belief and attachement/identification is the very root (the origin) of those emotions. Thus, they still possess the seeds and inclinations to manifest them again in the future and so the gods in Rupadhatu and Arupyadhatu may again fall in the lower realms. We must bear in mind that untill the root of negative emotions has been completely destroyed by the realization of perfect Enlightenment one cannot attain liberation from samsara.

In the World of Form (Rupadhatu) there are four spheres of heavenly realms, as follows:

The First Dhyana, which contains:
1. Heaven of the Councilors of Brahma (Brahmaparisadya)
2. Heaven of the High Priests of Brahma (Brahmapurohita)
3. Heaven of Great Brahma (Mahabrahman)

Some Brahma gods from the first Dhyana Heaven in the World of Form may experience the illusion of being all-powerful creators of the universe. About this kind of delusion brought upon them (and upon human beings who believe in them) by Maras, I discussed at lenght in the chapter "There is no supreme god or creator in the Buddha Dharma" from my book, *The True Teaching on*

Amida Buddha and His Pure Land[143]. Please read it carefully as I gave there many quotes from Shakyamuni Buddha himself.

The Second Dhyana, which contains:
1. Heaven of Lesser Light (Paritta-abha)
2. Heaven of Infinite Light (Apramana-abha)
3. Heaven of Supreme Light (Abhasvara)

The Third Dhyana, which contains:
1. Heaven of Lesser Purity (Parittasubha)
2. Heaven of Infinite Purity (Apramanasubha)
3. Heaven of Universal Purity (Śubhakrtsna)

The Fourth Dhyana, which contains:
1. Cloudless Heaven (Anabhraka)
2. Merit-producing Heaven (Punyaprasava)
3. Heaven of Greater Fruits (Brhatphala)
4. Heaven Free of Trouble (Abrha)
5. Heaven without Affliction (Atapa)
6. Heaven of Excellent Viewing (Sudrsa)
7. Heaven of Excellent Observation (Sudarsana)
8. Highest Heaven (Akanistha)

In the World of Non-form (Arupyadhatu) there are four heavenly realms:

Abode of Boundless Space (akasa-anantya-ayatana)

---

[143] *The True Teaching on Amida Buddha and His Pure Land*, by Josho Adrian Cirlea, Dharma Lion Publications, Craiova, 2015, p. 18

Abode of Boundless Consciousness (vijnana-anantya-ayatana)
Abode of Nothingness (akincanya-ayatana)
Abode of Neither Thought nor Non-thought (naiva-samjna-na-asamjna-ayatana)

The sufferings of the gods in the World of Desire (Kamadhatu) are of three types:
1) the suffering of dying and falling to lower realms, 2) the suffering of anxiety, and 3) the suffering of being cut, gashed, killed, and banished

1) The suffering of dying and falling to lower realms. No matter what sensual pleasures the gods in Kamadhatu experience, they will also die when the karma which brought them into their realms is exhausted. It is said that the suffering of dying in the realm of the gods is greater than in any other realm. Why is that? To die in the realm of hells or pretas means to be released from those spheres of extreme pain and a chance to be reborn in higher places, but who would really like to abandon the most beautiful realm filled with intoxicating pleasure and hapiness, where one has a perfect body and everything his heart desires?

Bodhisattva Nagarjuna said:

"Know that even Brahma himself,
After achieving happiness free from attachment
In his turn will endure ceaseless suffering

As fuel for the fires of the Hell of Ultimate Torment."[144]

"Although the deities have great pleasure in heaven,
The suffering of dying there is even greater than that.
The wise who understand this cease to create
Attachments for the perishable heavens."[145]

Before dying the gods experience the trauma of the five signs of death, as Nagarjuna described in the same text:

"Their bodies turn an unattractive color,
Their cushions become uncomfortable,
Their flower garlands wilt, and their clothing smells;
An unaccustomed sweat breaks out over their bodies.

The five signs that signal the deities in heaven,
Foretelling their death and departure therefrom,
Are similar to the signs
That foretell death for humans on earth."[146]

Even if the signs that fortell the death of gods may not seem extraordinary at first reading, please bear in mind that until those signs appear, their bodies were always fresh and healthy for many thousands of years, never smelled bad, never produced sweat, etc. So, its one thing to be human and have the above problems all the time,

---

[144] Nagarjuna as quoted in *Words of My Perfect Teacher*, by Patrul Rinpoche, revised edition, Padmakara Translation Group, Shambhala, Boston, 1998, p.94

[145] *Letter to a Friend*, as quoted in *The Great Treatise on the Stages of the Path to Enlightenment*, volume I, by Tsong-kha-pa, Snow Lion Publications, Ithaca, New York, p. 293

[146] *Idem*, p. 293 - 294.

and another to live happily like a god for many thousands of years in which only one minute of their life may be a hundred years of human life, and suddenly experience the five signs of death. And it is said in some texts that the time before dying, in which the gods experience the five signs and contemplate their falling into the lower realms, also lasts many years. During this time all the other gods leave them completely alone, being disgusted with the sight of their decay, and so the dying deity suffers enormously.

Master Genshin described the sufferings experienced by the gods from the World of Desire (Kamadhatu) when they approach death and gave us the example of those inhabiting the Trayastrimsa[147] (Heaven of the Thirty-three Gods)[148]:

"Even though the pleasures of these beings are boundless, when life comes to an end they cannot escape the pain of the Five Decays. The first is the fading of the crown of flowers. Second, the heavenly weather clothing becomes soiled. Third, sweat flows from the body. Fourth, the eyes often grow dizzy. And fifth, the place of living no longer gives enjoyment. These are called the Five Decays.

---

[147] Trāyastrimśa is Toriten in Japanese.
[148] He gives that example on the basis of the *Sutra of the Six Paramitas (Roku-haramitsu-kyo)*. This sutra was also named *Dai Rishu Ropparamitta, Ropparamitsu-kyo*, or *Liu-po-lo-mi-ching* in Chinese. It was translated from Sanskrit into Chinese in 788 by the monk Prajna.

When we meet with these sufferings we are disliked and cast off by the family of heavenly maidens. It is pitiful to roll around among the bushes and trees weeping and grieving. At such a time the victim cries out, saying: 'I was loved constantly by all the heavenly maidens and why is it that now they love me no longer? They have flung me away like grass and do not care for me in the least. Now there is nothing on which I can rely. Who is there to save me? Leaving the palace castle of Zenken, my life here must come to an end. There is no hope of seeing Teishaku[149] on his treasure throne. It is difficult to behold the glory of Shushoden[150] and doubtful whether I can ever again ride on the treasure elephant of Shakuten[151]. I shall never again gaze on the flowers of Shushaen. Never again shall I sit at the sake feast of Zorinen, nor play and linger in Kwankien. Sitting on the smooth stone of the white jewel under the Goba tree is a pleasure no longer possible. I can think no longer about bathing in the waters of Shushochi. I shall never again eat the Four Sweets and I alone am denied hearing the Five Glorious Kinds of Music. How sad that I alone must meet this fate! Oh, have mercy on me and save my life! But for a moment longer, I pray grant me this pleasure and let me not fall down on Mount Meru or into Bassho sea! But though I utter these prayers for help there is no one to save."

---

[149] Teishaku is Sakra (Indra), the ruler of the Heaven of the Thirty-three Gods (Trāyastrimśa).

[150] Shushoden and Shushaen, Zorinen, Kwankien, Goba tree, Shushochi are places and various elements of the Heaven of the Thirty-three Gods.

[151] Shakuten is the same as Tesihaku (Sakra/Indra).

Bodhisattva Nagarjuna also said about the falling of the gods:

"They must take leave of the divine worlds.
If their merit has run out,
Then, powerless, they will become
Animals, hungry ghosts, or denizens of hell."[152]

2) The suffering of anxiety
Depending on the merits they acumuated in previous lives, the gods in the World of Desire receive various pleasures and desirable objects. Thus, some have more than others, which causes those with lesser merits to become anxious and suffer.

3) The suffering of being cut, gashed, killed, and banished
Because of the wars they fight with asuras (demigods) they are often hurt in many ways. However, whenever they are injured their body parts regenerate with the exception of the head, as gods in the World of Desire can be killed only by cutting their heads. Some weaker gods are often banished from their places by the more powerful ones.

Bodhisattva Vasubandhu also described other kinds of suffering related with deities:

"Deities who indulge in sensual pleasures[153]

---

[152] *Letter to a Friend*, as quoted in *The Great Treatise on the Stages of the Path to Enlightenment*, volume I, by Tsong-kha-pa, Snow Lion Publications, Ithaca, New York, p. 294

*Are not happy in mind -
They are burned by an inner fire
Sparked by the infection of sensual desire.*

*How can there be happiness
For those whose minds are distracted?
Since their minds are not under control
And undistracted even for a moment,
They are by nature disturbed and agitated.
They will never be calm -
Like a fire that has wood for fuel
And that rages, whipped by the wind."*[154]

He also said:

*"They are like invalids, not long recovered
From an illness, who eat improperly and get sick
again."*[155]

The gods in the World of Form (Rupadhatu) and World of Non-Form (Arupyadhatu) do not experience the sufferings of the deities in the World of Desire (Kamadhatu), but they also die while still having subtle afflictions and osbscurations. As I said previously, they have not freed themselves from the belief and

---

[153] Gods in the World of Desire (Kamadhatu).
[154] *Sambhara - parikatha (Discussion of the Requisite Collections*, as quoted in *The Great Treatise on the Stages of the Path to Enlightenment*, volume I, by Tsong-kha-pa, Snow Lion Publications, Ithaca, New York, p. 294
[155] *The Great Treatise on the Stages of the Path to Enlightenment*, volume I, by Tsong-kha-pa, Snow Lion Publications, Ithaca, New York, p. 294

attachment to the false ego, so the root of negative emotions is still there even if they kept them hidden by being immersed in meditative absorbtion. Thus, not being liberated from samsara, they have no control over the course of their future karma and when the reservoir of merits that brought them in those high celestial abodes is exhausted, they fall again in lower realms.
Bodhisattva Vasubandhu said:

"Those in the form or formless realms
Are beyond the suffering of pain and the suffering of change.
By nature they have the bliss of meditative concentration;
They remain motionless for an eon.
But even this is most assuredly not liberation;
After they have counted on it, they will again fall.
Though it may seem as though they have transcended
The turbulence of the miserable realms,
Yet, like birds soaring in the sky,
They cannot stay forever, though they try -
Like an arrow shot with the strength of a child,
They will fall back down in the end.

Just as butter lamps that burn for a long time
Are in fact perishing in every moment,
They are afflicted by the changes of
The suffering of conditionality."[156]

---

[156] *Sambhara - parikatha (Discussion of the Requisite Collections*, as quoted in *The Great Treatise on the Stages of the Path to Enlightenment*, volume I, by Tsong-kha-pa, Snow Lion Publications, Ithaca, New York, p. 295

7. Contemplating the suffering of the intermediate state (bardo)

After describing each of the six realms of samsaric existence, I find it important to also explain the intermediate state between death and the next rebirth (*antarabhava* in Sanskrit, *bardo* in Tibetan)[157]. All beings pass through this state, which is itself filled with various dangers and suffering, depending on the individual karma. But first, let me say a few words about the process of dying.

Not all beings die the same way. Those who cultivated virtue and who die with a virtuous mind, that is, while remembering their good deeds or focusing on good thoughts, may see various pleasant images as though in a dream. Their death is comfortable and do not feel too much pain in body. On the other hand, those who did evil deeds and who die with an unvirtuous and attached mind experience immense suffering when leaving their bodies:

"When those who are currently cultivating nonvirtue die, they experience signs foretelling the effects of the nonvirtue they have engaged in. As if in a nightmare, many unpleasant images appear to them. [...] When those who have committed serious nonvirtuous actions observe

---

[157] In this chapter I do not intend to offer a complete and detailed explanation of the dying process and the subsequent intermediary state, but only to point out some of its basic aspects and to encourage my readers to avoid it by entrusting themselves to Amida Buddha since this very life, thus entering from now in the category of those assured of birth in the Pure Land after death.

these unpleasant signs, they experience physical pain and their hair stands on end. They shake their hands and feet, void urine and excrement, reach up toward the sky, roll their eyes back, drool, and more. If they have been moderate in their nonvirtue, then not all of these things will happen - some will and some will not."[158]

Those who were somehow neutral in cultivating virtue or non-virtue or their mind does not dwell on neither virtue and non-virtue at the moment of death, they have neither pain nor pleasure when they die.

The consciousness or the mind-stream leaves the body in different ways for different people:

"Among those who are currently cultivating nonvirtue, consciousness leaves the body coming down from the upper parts, which become cold first. When it reaches the heart, it leaves the body. The consciousness of someone who is currently cultivating virtue leaves coming up from the lower parts and the body becomes cold from the lower parts. In both cases consciousness leaves from the heart.
The point at which consciousness first enters the fertilized ovum becomes the body's heart; consciousness finally leaves the body from where it first entered. Given that, at first the heat of the body either descends from the

---

[158] *The Great Treatise on the Stages of the Path to Enlightenment*, volume I, by Tsong-kha-pa, Snow Lion Publications, Ithaca, New York, p. 292-293. It should be noted that Tsong-kha-pa was greatly inspired by Bodhisattva Vasubandhu in his explanations of the intermediate states that I quote in this chapter.

upper parts and gathers in the heart or ascends from the lower parts and gathers in the heart."[159]

So, the consciousness or mind-stream leaves the body from the heart region, enters the intermediate state and then goes to its future place of rebirth. However, we should not think that going to a future place of rebirth is a voluntary process, that is, the bardo being does not look for its next birthplace as if chosing or deciding where to go. In fact, **his own karma pushes him in the direction of his next birth, like a strong wind who cannot be resisted**.

Bodhisattva Vasubandhu, our 2nd Patriarch, put great efforts in explaining and defending the existence of the intermediary state[160], by quoting various sutras and offering many logical Dharmic explanations. He said:

"Scripture also proves the existence of an intermediate being. [...] We read in the Sutra: 'Three conditions are necessary in order for a son or daughter to be born: the woman must be in good health and fertile, the pair must be united, and a gandharva must be ready.' **What is the gandharva if not an intermediate being?**"[161]

He also said:

---

[159] *The Great Treatise on the Stages of the Path to Enlightenment*, volume I, by Tsong-kha-pa, Snow Lion Publications, Ithaca, New York, p. 309
[160] See for example, *Abhidharmakossabhasyam*, English translation by Leo M. Pruden; Berkeley, Calif, Asian Humanities Press, 1991; vol 2, p 383-401
[161] *Idem*, p 386

"What is an intermediate being, and an intermediate existence? Intermediate existence, which inserts itself between existence at death and existence at birth, not having arrived at the location where it should go, cannot be said to be born. Between death - that is, the five skandhas of the moment of death - and arising - that is, the five skandhas of the moment of rebirth - **there is found an existence - a "body" of five skandhas -** *that goes to the place of rebirth.* **This existence between two realms of rebirth (gati) is called intermediate existence.**"[162]

As explained at a previous chapter, all the physical and mental elements of a being are classified in five types of skandhas ("agregates"): 1) form (a generic name for all kinds of matter and the body), 2) feeling or sensation, 3) perception, 4) mental formations (mental states), 5) consciousness or mind.

A gandharva or a person passing through the intermediate state has all the five aggregates (skandhas). Although his body is not composed of flesh and bones like ours, we may definitely call his form a body as it has perfectly developed organs[163]. This body or form looks like the body he will have in his next rebirth.

Vasubandhu said:

---

[162] *Idem*, p 383

[163] The consciousness cannot stay without a body, so it assumes a bardo body, which is very similar to a dream body. When dreaming we are not just naked minds, but also have a body, and the same happens in the intermediate state.

*"What is the form of an intermediate being?
An intermediate being has the form of the being of the realm of rebirth to come after his conception[164].*

*The action that projects the gati or the realm of rebirth is the same action that projects the intermediate existence by which one goes to this realm of rebirth. As a consequence, antarabhava or intermediate existence has the form of the future realm of rebirth towards which he is going. [...]
The dimensions of an intermediate being are those of a child of five or six years of age, but his organs are perfectly developed.[165]*

Not only the organs of an intermediate being (gandharva) are complete[166], but he can also move through any material object:

"His organs are complete. [...] No one can resist him. [...] Even a diamond is not impenetrable to him."[167]

He has other supernatural capacities too, like being capable of moving through space:

---

[164] Some Masters say that the intermediate being looks very similar with his previous life at the begining of bardo and then, as the time passes, he starts to look more and more with the being he will become in his future birth.
[165] *Abhidharmakossabhasyam*, English translation by Leo M. Pruden; Berkeley, Calif, Asian Humanities Press, 1991; vol 2, p 390
[166] It is said that if a being was blind or death during life, in the bardo he can see and hear, etc. All his sensory faculties are complete.
[167] *Abhidharmakossabhasyam*, English translation by Leo M. Pruden; Berkeley, Calif, Asian Humanities Press, 1991; vol 2, p 392

"He is filled with the impetus of the supernormal power of action.
He is a 'karmarddhivegavan': endowed (van) with the impetus (vega) which belongs to supernatural power (rddhi) - that is, the movement through space - which issues from action (karman). The Buddhas themselves cannot stop him because he is endowed with the force of action."[168]

Moving through space may seem a joyful thing, but in fact, it is very troublesome for the intermediate being. If when he was alive he could let his mind wander into any direction, but the body stayed in one place, during the bardo (intermediate state), if his mind thinks about a particular place, he will automatically be there. Then again, just when he arrives, he will go to another place at the next thought. Thus, an unstable mind experiences a constant and painful changing of scenery. Being carried in many places like a feather blown by the wind, the bardo person might feel confusion, frustration and fear.

Another capacity of an intermediate being is seeing at a great distance and perhaps through various objects:
"It possesses, by virtue of its actions, the divine eye."[169]

This 'divine eye' should not be understood as a divine eye possesed by a Buddha or a very advanced Bodhisattva which is obtained through higher knowledge or purity, but just as a supernatural eye of the intermediary state.

---

[168] *Ibidem*
[169] *Idem*, p 394

The Buddhas or Bodhisattvas can see him with their divine eyes, as Vasubandhu explains:

"He is seen by the pure divine eye, that is, by the divine eye that is obtained through higher knowledge (abhijna), for this eye is very pure. He is not seen by a natural divine eye or a divine eye obtained through birth, such as the divine eye of the gods."[170]

He is also seen by and can see other intermediate beings of his class, that is, other gandharvas who will go to the same places of rebirth as him:

"He is seen by the intermediate beings of the class to which he belongs".[171]

However, some gandharvas (intermediate beings) might see gandharvas from other classes, too:

"According to other masters, a heavenly intermediate being sees all intermediate beings; a human intermediate being sees all intermediate beings with the exception of heavenly intermediate beings, and so on."[172]

A gandharva can also eat:

---

[170] *Abhidharmakossabhasyam*, English translation by Leo M. Pruden; Berkeley, Calif, Asian Humanities Press, 1991; vol 2, p 392
[171] *Ibidem*
[172] *Ibidem*

"Does an intermediate being of Kamadhatu eat, like the other beings of Kamadhatu, solid food? Yes, but not coarse food. **It eats odors***.*
From whence it gets its name of gandharva, 'he who eats (arvati) odors (gandham)'. The meanings of the roots are multiple: 'arv', if one takes it in the sense of 'to go,' justifies 'he who goes to eat odors' (arvati gacchati bhoktum). A gandharva of low rank eats unpleasant odors; a gandharva of high rank eats pleasant odors."[173]

The intermediate state appears differently to different types of intermediate beings. The *Descent into the Womb Sutra* says:

"For someone who is to be reborn a hell-being, the intermediate state is like a charred log; for one to be reborn an animal it is like smoke; for one to be reborn a hungry ghost, it is like water; for one to be reborn a deity of the desire realm and a human, it is like gold; for one to be reborn a deity of the form realm, it is white."[174]
The existence of a gandharva (intermediate being) is short, as Bodhisattva Vasubandhu explained:

"How long does an intermediate being exist?

---

[173] *Idem*, p 393
[174] *The Great Treatise on the Stages of the Path to Enlightenment*, volume I, by Tsong-kha-pa, Snow Lion Publications, Ithaca, New York, p. 310

There is no fixed rule. It lasts as long as it does not encounter the coming together of the causes necessary for its rebirth."[175]

However, all the sacred texts that treat this topic agree that it does not last longer than seven weeks (49 days) during which he certainly finds the conditions for rebirth.

"The Bhadanta Vasumitra[176] *says: An intermediate being lasts seven days. [...] Other scholars say that it lasts seven weeks. According to others, if the causes have not come together, the intermediate being is born in conditions analogous to those where he would have been reborn. Cattle are not born during the rains, nor black bears in winter, nor horses in summer. But on the other hand, there is no season for buffalos, etc. The intermediary being who, if it is the season of rains, would be reborn a cow, is reborn a buffalo; in the same way a jackal instead of a dog, a brown bear instead of a black bear, or an ass instead of a horse."*[177]

---

[175] *Abhidharmakossabhasyam*, English translation by Leo M. Pruden; Berkeley, Calif, Asian Humanities Press, 1991; vol 2, p 393
[176] Vasumitra (or Sumitra,Vasumitra 世友 (n.d.) (Skt; Jpn Seu or Seyu): The monk who led the Fourth Buddhist Council in Kashmir around the second century and helped compile The Great Commentary on the Abhidharma. Chinese Buddhist Encyclopedia, http://www.chinabuddhismencyclopedia.com/en/index.php/Vasumitra
[177] *Abhidharmakossabhasyam*, English translation by Leo M. Pruden; Berkeley, Calif, Asian Humanities Press, 1991; vol 2, p 393-394

Also, if an intermediate being *"does not find the conditions of rebirth within seven days, he can assume another body witthin the intermediate state."*[178]

His karma and his destination can change, too: *"a being of the intermediate state that is to be reborn as a deity, for instance, may die after seven days and either again reach the intermediate state of a deity or else reach the intermediate state of a human or some other form. This is possible because a change in its karma can transform the seeds for its intermediate state. The same holds for other beings of the intermediate state as well."*[179]

This aspect is extremely important because it shows how unpredictable the intermediate state can be. One never knows what winds of karma will blow on the poor gandharva (intermediate being) and change his course from a pleasant to an unpleasant rebirth. His own thoughts but also the thoughts and actions of others surrounding his dead body can become great obstacles during the intermediate state. An outburst of anger when seeing his relatives doing something against his wish or the arise of various attachements may generate the seeds of going in the direction of the lower realms.

When the bardo process begins, the conscience gets out of the body, of course, but this does not mean one is always aware that one is dead. The bardo can be better

---

[178] *The Great Treatise on the Stages of the Path to Enlightenment*, volume I, by Tsong-kha-pa, Snow Lion Publications, Ithaca, New York, p. 311
[179] *Ibidem*

understood if we compare it to the dream state. When asleep, we sometimes know we are dreaming while other times we don't know and act like that dream is reality. In the same way, during bardo, we can realize we are dead and some other times we forget. Also, just like in a dream, the appearances and experiences change many times, and anything can disturb the intermediate being. Thus, if the environment surrounding one's death is very emotional with people crying, remembering him and his life's events with strong attachement, calling his name, or criticizing and hating him, then the consciousness might be affected by giving rise to negative thoughts. This is very dangerous for the bardo being and may be a great obstacle for a good rebirth. It is exactly because of this that relatives must maintain a peaceful and religious atmosphere around the body of a dead person when it's still held in the house and also during the entire 49 days of bardo. If the dead person was not a faithful devotee of Amida Buddha during his lifetime and he was not born in the Pure Land immediately after death, then his karmic destiny is very insecure.

The rebirth (reincarnation) appears in the following way for those who are to be born from egg or womb:

"How does reincarnation take place?
The mind (mati) troubled by defilements, goes, through its desire for sex, to the place of its realm of rebirth.

An intermediate being is produced with a view to going to the place of its realm of rebirth where it should go. It possesses, by virtue of its actions, the divine eye. Even though distant he sees the place of his rebirth. There he sees his father and mother united. His mind is troubled by the effects of sex and hostility. When the intermediate being is male, it is gripped by a male desire with regard to the mother; when it is female, it is gripped by a female desire with regard to the father; and, inversely, it hates either the father, or the mother, whom it regards as either a male or a female rival. As it is said in the Prajnapti, 'Then either a mind of lust, or a mind of hatred is produced in the gandharva (intermediate being).'

When the mind is thus troubled by these two erroneous thoughts, it attaches itself through the desire for sex to the place where the organs are joined together, imagining that it is he with whom they unite. Then the impurities of semen and blood[180] is found in the womb; the intermediate being, enjoying its pleasures, installs itself there. Then the skandhas harden; the intermediate being perishes; and birth arises that is called "reincarnation" (pratisamdhi). [...]

It is in this manner that beings who are born from wombs and eggs go to the places of their rebirth (gati)."[181]

---

[180] This should be read as the union of male sperm with female egg (ovum). According to the Buddha Dharma life in human form starts at the moment of conception when the conscience of a being in the intermediate state (Gandharva) enters the cell formed after the union of male sperm with female egg.

[181] *Abhidharmakossabhasyam*, English translation by Leo M. Pruden; Berkeley, Calif, Asian Humanities Press, 1991; vol 2, p 394-396

Rebirth for hell beings and hungry ghosts (pretas) may also occur like this:

"If the being of the intermediate state does not have a desire to go to a birthplace, it will not migrate there, and having not done so, will not be reborn there. Take, for example, the case of those who have committed and accumulated karma for rebirth in a hell, like those who have no vow against activities such as butchering sheep or poultry or marketing hogs. In these peoples' intermediate state they see, as if in a dream, sheep and such at their future birthplace, and rush there, driven by their delight in their former habits. Then anger is aroused at the forms which attracted them to the birthplace, at which point their intermediate state ends, and they are reborn.

Hungry ghosts with goiters, and others who are similar to hell beings, take rebirth in a like manner.

If the being of the intermediate state is to be reborn as an animal, hungry ghost, human, desire-realm deity (kammadathu), or form-realm deity, it observes at its birthplace delightful beings similar to itself. Then, conceiving a liking and a desire for that place, it migrates there and becomes angry upon seeing the birthplace, at which time its intermediate state ends, and it is reborn."[182]

---

[182] *The Great Treatise on the Stages of the Path to Enlightenment*, volume I, by Tsong-kha-pa, Snow Lion Publications, Ithaca, New York, p. 313

Bodhisattva Vasubandhu also said:

"For other beings, say the masters of the Abhidharma, the modes vary according to the case.
Other go in their desire for odor or in their desire for residence. Beings which arise from moisture go to the place of their rebirth through their desire for its odors: these are pure or impure by reason of their actions. Apparitional beings[183], go through their desire for residence there.

But how can one desire a residence in hell? The mind of an intermediate being is troubled by lust and hatred, as we have seen, when it goes to be reincarnated in a womb. In the present case, an intermediate being is also troubled in mind and misunderstands. He is tormented by the cold of rain and wind: he sees a place burning with hot fires and through his desire for warmth, he runs there. Or he is tormented by the heat of the sun and hot winds: he sees a cold place of frozen fires, and through his desire for coolness, he runs there. According to the ancient masters, he sees these things in order to experience the retribution of actions that should be retributed in hell; he sees beings similar to him and he runs to the place where they are.

Intermediate heavenly beings - those who go towards a heavenly realm of rebirth - go high, like one rising up from a seat. Humans, animals, pretas, and intermediate beings go in the manner in which humans, etc, go. Beings

---

[183] Apparitional beings are hell dwellers, pretas (hungry ghosts) and gods or heavenly beings.

in hell hang from their feet. As the stanza says, 'Those who insult sages (rishis), ascetics and penitents fall into hell head first.'"[184]

Following the explanations of Bodhisattva Vasubandhu, Master Tsong-kha-pa says the same:

"In his commentary on this, Vasubandhu explains that if the being of the intermediate state is to be reborn from heat and moisture, it craves smells, while if it is to be reborn spontaneously, it desires a place and is subsequently reborn there. It further explains that if this being is to be reborn in a hot hell, it craves warmth, while if it is to be bom in a cold hell, it longs to be cool."[185]

*

We should contemplate on the above descriptions of the intermediate state and imagine ourselves there. Even during our present life we wander in all directions with distracted minds, thus causing ourselves various psychological problems. However, the power of every thought and delusion becomes ten times stronger when in the bardo, so imagine the danger we may experience there. Let's pretend that some can be succesful in achieving liberation in the bardo, but can you, the reader

---

[184] *Abhidharmakossabhasyam*, English translation by Leo M. Pruden; Berkeley, Calif, Asian Humanities Press, 1991; vol 2, p 396-397

[185] *The Great Treatise on the Stages of the Path to Enlightenment*, volume I, by Tsong-kha-pa, Snow Lion Publications, Ithaca, New York, p. 313

of these lines, be so sure that you are one of them? Even for very advanced practitioners who prepared themselves all their lives to practice in the bardo, there is still plenty of room for errors. But there is no possibility for failure to become a Buddha in the Pure Land if you rely on Amida, because there is not even the slightest trace of your own limited personal power involved in this process. **If you have entrusted yourself to Amida Buddha during your life, then His Infinite Power has been at work all the time, destroying the roots of your karma, and now, when dying, it continues to be active and it will take you safely to His Pure Land. Thus, while every unenlightened sentient being has to pass through bardo when they die, the Amida devotees don't experience this intermediate state.** Shinran Shonin said:

*"Through the karmic power of the great Vow, the person who has realized true and real shinjin (faith in Amida Buddha) naturally is in accord with the cause of birth in the Pure Land and **is drawn by the Buddha's karmic power**; hence the going is easy, and ascending to and attaining the supreme great Nirvana is without limit."*[186]

He also said in one of his *Letters (Mattosho)*:

"I, for my own part, attach no significance to the condition, good or bad, of persons in their final moments. People in whom shinjin is determined do not doubt, and

---

[186] *Notes on the Inscriptions on Sacred Scrolls - The Collected Works of Shinran*, Shin Buddhism Translation Series, Jodo Shinshu Hongwanji-ha, Kyoto, 1997, p. 496-497

so abide among the truly settled. For this reason their end also - even for those ignorant and foolish and lacking in wisdom - is a happy one."[187]

These blessed words should give us true relief and assurance when we think about death and the intermediary state. No matter if we die well, in our bed, or in the street like homeless persons, no matter if we feel good or bad, if we smile and die peacefully with the appearance of wise people or we cry because of pain, no matter if our death makes a good impression or not, no matter if we die of old age or in our youth, we are accepted exactly as we are and we will be born in the Pure Land because of Amida's Compassion.

In His Primal Vow, Amida Buddha did not mention a special condition in which we have to die in order to be born in the Pure Land - He just promised that those beings who entrust to Him, wish to be born in His land and say His Name will be born there.

In Jodo Shinshu we are saved during this life, that is, we enter the stage of non-retrogression ("truly settled") or the stage of those assured of Nirvana in the moment we entrust ourselves to Amida Buddha, and after death we are born in the Pure Land where we become Buddhas.

Even after we receive shinjin (faith in Amida Buddha) we continue to live our lives like ordinary people, filled with blind passions and illusions, and we can die like ordinary people because of the problems of ordinary

---

[187] *Idem*, p. 531

people. But this very ordinary person is already "received and never abandoned" by the Compassion of Amida Buddha and so his end becomes a happy one.

Question:
Can a person who did not entrust to Amida Buddha during his life, change his mind and entrust while in the intermediate state?

Answer:
I do not recall any passage from Shinran, Rennyo, Honen or other Patriarch of our lineage in which liberation through faith while in bardo was mentioned, but I think its possible. If the intermediate being hears about Amida Buddha's salvation from a Dharma friend who stays near his dead body and encourages him to take refuge in Amida or if he remembers a teaching about Amida he received during his life and decides to entrust to Him, say His Name and wish to go to His Pure Land, then I am sure he can reach that land[188]. However, I do not advise anybody to wait until bardo to entrust to Amida Buddha, when he can do it so easily here. One can never know what karma and ignorance can manifest during the intermediate state that may prevent a person without faith to remember or hear about Amida Buddha. So please, do not misunderstand my answer and try your best to solve your doubts while you are still alive so that you can automatically reach the Pure Land when you die.

---

[188] Into my opinion a bardo being who entrusts to Amida Buddha dies in the bardo state and is instantly reborn in the Pure Land.

Concluding thoughts on the suffering of samsaric existence

As we have seen in the description of the six realms, there is absolutely no place in samsara without suffering. Everything is a cause for suffering, everything is multyplying suffering, and everything, even the intoxicating pleasures of the gods, contain the seed of suffering.

"Beings in hell suffer from hell-fire,
Pretas suffer from hunger and thirst,
Animals suffer from being eaten by each other,
Humans suffer from having a short life,
Asuras suffer from wars and quarrels,
And the gods suffer from their own mindlessness.
In samsara there is never a pinpoint of happiness."[189]

Some say that life in the gods realm is more desirable because of the immense pleasure we can find there. However, I would like to ask you, what if somebody offers you the most intense party with the best drinks, women or men, on a luxurious yacht, for three days, on the condition that after the party you will be burnt to death? Would you accept the deal? Would the pain you'll suffer by being burnt to death worth the sweet and

---

[189] Shakyamuni Buddha, *Saddharma Smrity-upasthana Sutra (Sutra of Sublime Dharma of Clear Recollection)* as quoted in *Words of My Perfect Teacher*, by Patrul Rinpoche, revised edition, Padmakara Translation Group, Shambhala, Boston, 1998, p.94

transient pleasure of three nights? This is similar with the various distractions of the gods realms. When their time come, gods themselves suffer intensely, as I aleady described above, in the section dedicated to them. If one reaches the highest point of the wheel of samsara, one will surely fall from there to the lower part after spending one's karmic merits in intoxicating pleasures. Just like a rich guy enters a casino with the attitude of a great lord, and is treated well by everybody, if he looses all his wealth at gambling, he will be thrown away like a beggar at the end of the programe.

There is a signficant story of the monk Nanda who was very much attached to his wife and had no aspiration to renounce the world. Seeing this, Shakyamuni Buddha miraculously took him to a mountain where he showed him a one-eyed monkey. He asked him: "Tell me Nanda, who do you find more beautiful, this monkey or your wife?" Nanda replied immediately, "My wife, of course!" Then the Buddha transported him to a realm of the gods where He showed him many beautiful mansions where each god lived together with his assembly of young godesses and enjoyed many pleasures and abundance. Then he took him to a palace where there were many goddesses but no god. When Nanda asked why, a godess answered, "there is a person in the human world, a disciple of the Buddha whose name is Nanda and who practices the Way. The karma he thus accumulates will make him reborn in this palace where we will serve him faithfully." Nanda was very joyful and when asked by the Buddha who he now thinks is more beautiful, his wife or the goddesses, he answered without any hesitation: "the

goddesses are far more beautiful! My wife cannot even compare herself with them."
Then, when he returned to the human world, Nanda practiced the Way even more seriously so that he does not lose the chance to be reborn with the beautiful godesses.

After some time the Buddha asked him if he wants to go with him to visit the hells. Nanda agreed and he was transported there by the Buddha's miraculus power. While visiting the various hells and seeing the horror and pain of the beings born there, he came across an empty pot filled with blazing fire and a number of hells tormentors around it. When he asked why is the pot empty, a hell tormentor answered: "we are waiting for a person called Nanda, who is now practicing the Way in the human realm in order to be born among the gods. After he enjoys many hundreds of years in that celestial place, his merits will run out and he will be reborn here." This terrified Nanda so much that he pondered more deeply on the characteristics of samsara. Then, after realizing that there is no sense to aspire for a happiness that ends in the flame of hells, he awoke the aspiration to escape from all samsaric existence.

We should really take to heart the story of Nanda and contemplate deeply the nature of samsara. Even if we did not see with our own eyes the lower or higher realms, a picture or the many descriptions made by Shakyamuni Buddha and the masters of various lineages should be enough to scare the hell out of us and make us wish to escape from it

Thus, let us never forget that in samsara 1) **there is no certainty**, 2) **we can never find satisfaction**, 3) **we are born and we die repeatedly, changing bodies after bodies ad infinitum**, 4) **on the wheel of samsara we will always go down after we go high**, and 5) **we have no true companions**. All samsaric beings meet with these five general types of suffering.

1) What does it mean to have no certainty in samsara?

It means for example, that we are never certain our dear ones from today we'll remain dear to us in the next lives. Of course, we would like to be able to meet again with our good friends, parents, children or wife after we die. But if we meet again with them in another life and still we are not Buddhas, then this meeting might be of no real benefit to them or to us. It can even become a meeting of pain and sorrow, in which we surely won't recognize them. Because of our deluded minds, we might harm them or make them run from us.

We and our loved ones have different karma and after this life we will take different forms, but because of attachments to one another we can still be close in space and time. For example, one of us might be born in the next life as a human being, while the other (wife, husband, parent, friend) can be born as an animal. Due to attachment he (or she) can live around our house, but because we cannot see our previous lives, we are not able to recognize him. We can think of him as just a close dog or cow, but we cannot really give him much benefit.

It can even be worse than this. In time our feelings for him/her or his feelings towards us may change and because of various circumstances love can turn into hate. People who are now in a love relation can hate each other after a few lives, or even in this life. So, until we become Buddhas, not only can we not give any benefit to our close ones, but we can actually make them sink even more in the ocean of suffering.

Bodhisattva Nagarjuna said:

*"For those in cyclic existence there are no certainties
Because fathers become sons, mothers become wives,
Enemies become friends,
And the converse happens as well."*[190]

Thus, if we truly care about them, we should make a commitment not to lose this life in vain, but to listen to the teaching again and again and receive faith in Amida Buddha. Only in this way, our aspiration to save all beings, especially those with whom we have karmic connections, will be fulfilled.

2) We can never find satisfaction in samsara

Bodhisattva Nagarjuna said:

*"Each of us has drunk more milk
Than would fill the four oceans; yet*

---

[190] *Letter to a Friend*, as quoted in *The Great Treatise on the Stages of the Path to Enlightenment*, volume I, by Tsong-kha-pa, Snow Lion Publications, Ithaca, New York, p. 281

*Those in cyclic existence who act as ordinary beings
Are intent on drinking still more than that."[191]*

Since the beginingless past we have tried many ways to satisfy our desires. We worked hard, fought hard, even killed or hurt others in order to find hapiness, but still never found it. Our unfulfilled desires and attachments needed a new vehicle with every new life, and so we continued to run into an endless variety of forms (bodies), trying desperately to satisfy them. This is why we must ask ourselves - when we'll finaly learn that there is no real satisfaction in samsara and in our samsaric pursuits? When we'll be finaly able to say - "STOP!" Why don't we get sick of this never ending sorrow?

*"Just as a leper tormented by maggots
Turns to fire for relief, but finds no peace,
So should you understand
Attachment to sensual pleasures."[192]*

Candragomin said in his *Letter to a Student (Sisya-lekha)*:
*"What being has not come into the world hundreds of times?
What pleasure has not already been experienced countless*

---

[191] *Letter to a Friend*, as quoted in *The Great Treatise on the Stages of the Path to Enlightenment*, volume I, by Tsong-kha-pa, Snow Lion Publications, Ithaca, New York, p. 282

[192] *Letter to a Friend* by Nagarjuna, as quoted in *The Great Treatise on the Stages of the Path to Enlightenment*, volume I, by Tsong-kha-pa, Snow Lion Publications, Ithaca, New York, p. 282

times?
What luxury, such as splendid white yak-tail fans, have they
not owned?
Yet, even when they possess something, their attachment continues to grow.

There is no suffering they have not experienced many times.
The things they desire do not satisfy them.
There is no living being that has not slept in their bellies.
So why do they not rid themselves of attachment to cyclic existence?"[193]

Master Asvagosha said:

"Again and again in hells
You drank boiling liquid copper -
So much that even the water in the ocean
Does not compare.

The filth you have eaten
As a dog and as a pig
Would make a pile far more vast
Than Meru, the king of mountains.
On account of losing loved ones and friends
You have shed so many tears
In the realms of cyclic existence
That the ocean could not contain them.

---

[193] *The Great Treatise on the Stages of the Path to Enlightenment*, volume I, by Tsong-kha-pa, Snow Lion Publications, Ithaca, New York, p. 283

*The heads that have been severed
From fighting one another,
If piled up, would
Reach beyond Brahma's heaven.*

*You have been a worm
And, having been ravenous, you ate so much sludge
That if it were poured into the great ocean
It would fill it completely."[194]*

Shakyamuni Buddha said:

*"Remember the infinite bodies which, in the past,
You wasted senselessly on account of desire;
As many times as there are grains of sand in the Ganges
You failed to please the Buddhas and ignored their teachings."[195]*

Shinran Shonin also said:

*"Under the guidance of Buddhas who appeared in this world,
Three times the sands of the Ganges in number,
We awakened the aspiration for supreme Enlightenment,*

---

[194] *Sokavinodana (Alleviating Sorrow)* by Asvagosha, as quoted in *The Great Treatise on the Stages of the Path to Enlightenment*, volume I, by Tsong-kha-pa, Snow Lion Publications, Ithaca, New York, p. 283

[195] *Ganda-vyuha Sutra (Array of Stalks Sutra)*, as quoted in *The Great Treatise on the Stages of the Path to Enlightenment*, volume I, by Tsong-kha-pa, Snow Lion Publications, Ithaca, New York, p. 284

But our self-power failed, and we continued to transmigrate."[196]

*"Were it not for the ship of Amida's Vow,
How could I cross the ocean of painful existence?*

*With minds full of malice and cunning, like snakes and scorpions,
We cannot accomplish good acts through self-power;
And unless we entrust ourselves to Amida's directing of virtue,
We will end without knowing shame or self-reproach"*.[197]

3) In samsara we are born and we die repeatedly, changing bodies after bodies ad infinitum

Bodhisattva Nagarjuna said:

*"Each of us has left a pile of bones
That would dwarf Mount Meru."*[198]

Shakyamuni Buddha also said:

---

[196] *Pure Land Hymns on the Right, Semblance and Last Dharma Ages*, The Collected Works of Shinran, http://shinranworks.com/hymns-in-japanese/hymns-of-the-dharma-ages/pure-land-hymns-on-the-right-semblance-and-last-dharma-ages
[197] *Shozomatsu Wasan*, The Collected Works of Shinran, Shin Buddhism Translation Series, Jodo Shinshu Hongwanji-ha, Kyoto, 1997, p.421-422
[198] *Letter to a Friend*, as quoted in *The Great Treatise on the Stages of the Path to Enlightenment*, volume I, by Tsong-kha-pa, Snow Lion Publications, Ithaca, New York, p. 284

"The bones of a single person wandering in Samsara would be a cairn, a pile, a heap as Mount Vepulla, were there a collector of these bones and were the collections not destroyed.
Longtime have you suffered the death of father and mother, of sons, daughters, brothers and sisters, and while you were thus suffering, you have verily shed tears upon this long way, more than there is water in the four oceans.
Long time did your blood flow by the loss of your heads when you were born as oxen, buffaloes. rams, goats, etc. Long time have you been caught as dacoits or highwaymen or adulterers, and through your being beheaded, verily more blood has flowed upon this long way than there is water in the four oceans.
And thus have you for long time undergone sufferings, undergone torment, undergone misfortune, and filled the graveyards full, verily long enough to be dissatisfied with every form of existence, long enough to turn away and free yourself from them all."[199]

"If someone took from this vast earth pellets the size of juniper berries and set them aside, saying, 'This is my mother, and this is my mother's mother,' then, monks, the clay of this vast earth would be exhausted, yet the line of matrilineal predecessors would not."[200]

---

[199] *Anguttara Nikaya* as translated by Venerable Narada Mahathera in his book, *The Buddha and His Teachings*, http://www.buddhism.org/Sutras/BuddhaTeachings/page_31.html
[200] Buddha Shakyamuni, as quoted in *The Great Treatise on the Stages of the Path to Enlightenment*, volume I, by Tsong-kha-pa, Snow Lion Publications, Ithaca, New York, p. 285

In the *Anguttara Nikaya* it is said:

"On one occasion the Venerable Sariputta was dwelling in Magadha, in the village Nalaka. On that occasion, Samandakani, a wandering ascetic, approached him and asked:
'What, friend Sariputta, is happiness, and what is suffering?'
'To be reborn, friend, is suffering; not to be reborn is happiness.'"[201]

4) On the wheel of samsara we will always go down after we go high

Bodhisattva Nagarjuna said:

"Having become Indra, worthy of the world's honor, you will
still fall
Once again to the earth because of the force of past karma.
Even having become a universal monarch,
You will once again become a slave for other beings in cyclic
existence.

Though you have long experienced the pleasures

---

[201] *Anguttara Nikaya - Discourses of the Buddha*, selected and translated from Pali by Nyanaponika Thera and Bhikku Bodhi, Buddhist Publication Society, Kandy, Sri Lanka, volume 3, page 19, https://www.urbandharma.org/pdf1/wh238AnguttaraNikaya3.pdf

Of caressing the breasts and waists of divine women,
You will once again encounter the unbearable sensations
Of the grinding, cutting, and flesh-tearing hell-devices.

Having dwelled long on the peak of Mount Meru,
Enjoying the pleasant touch of soft ground on your feet,
Imagine undergoing the unbearable pain
Of walking once again over hot coals and rotting corpses in hell.
Having frolicked in beautiful groves
And enjoyed the embraces of divine women,
You will arrive once again in the forests of hell, where the
leaves
Are swords that slice off ears, nose, hands, and legs.

Though you have entered the Gently Flowing River
With beautiful goddesses and golden lotuses,
You will plunge once more in hell into scalding water -
The unbearable waters of the Impassable River.

Having gained the great pleasures of a deity
In the realm of desire, or the detached happiness of Brahma,
You will once again become fuel for the fires
Of the Unrelenting Hell, suffering pain without respite.

Having been a deity of the sun or the moon,
Illuminating all the world with the light of your body,
You will return once more to dense, black darkness,

Where you cannot see even your own outstretched hand."[202]

It is said in the *Vinaya-vastu*:

*"The end of accumulated things is depletion.
The end of things that are high is a fall.
The end of meetings is separation.
The end of life is death."*[203]

5) In samsara we have no true companions

In *Bodhisattvacaryavatara* it is said:

*"This body comes forth whole, yet
The bones and flesh that accompany it
Will break apart and disperse. As this is so,
Why mention others, such as loved ones?*

*You are born alone.
Also you die alone.
As others cannot share your suffering,
Of what use is the hindrance of loved ones?"*[204]

---

[202] *Letter to a Friend*, as quoted in *The Great Treatise on the Stages of the Path to Enlightenment*, volume I, by Tsong-kha-pa, Snow Lion Publications, Ithaca, New York, p. 285-286

[203] *Vinaya-vastu (The Bases of Discipline)* as quoted in *The Great Treatise on the Stages of the Path to Enlightenment*, volume I, by Tsong-kha-pa, Snow Lion Publications, Ithaca, New York, p. 286

[204] *Bodhisattvacaryavatara (Engaging in the Bodhisattva Deeds)*, as quoted in *The Great Treatise on the Stages of the Path to Enlightenment*, volume I, by Tsong-kha-pa, Snow Lion Publications, Ithaca, New York, p. 287

Friends, family and loved ones are as fleeting as a crowd on market day. Now they are here with us, and the next time they are gone. Also, who can really take our pain when we are ill, when we get old or when we die? Even if they have empathy for us, they cannot suffer, get old or die in our place. Also, they cannot go to the samsaric destinations where we deserve to be reborn due to our karma. Please meditate on this!

*

After deeply contemplating the general sufferings of samsara and the specific sufferings of each of the six realms of samsaric existence and the bardo, our minds should naturaly turn toward Amida Dharma, the only path that affords passage in this dark age of the five defilements:

"To awaken aspiration and perform practices in this world
Is the Path of Sages and is termed self-power.
The present is the last Dharma-age; it is the world of the five defilements;
The Pure Land way alone affords passage."[205]

Then, we should make this promise to ourselves and to all mother sentient beings:

"I wish to abandon the body enclosed in the womb

---

[205] Shinran Shonin, *Hymn of the Two Gateways of Entrance and Emergence, The Collected Works of Shinran*, Shin Buddhism Translation Series, Jodo Shinshu Hongwanji-ha, Kyoto, 1997, p.628

*And attain birth in the Land of Peace and Bliss,
Where I will quickly behold Amida Buddha's
Body of boundless merits and virtues
And see many Tathagathas
And holy sages as well.
Having acquired the six supernatural powers,
I will continue to save suffering sentient beings
Until all their worlds throughout the universe are exhausted.
Such will be my vow.
After having thus made a vow, I take refuge in Amida Buddha
with sincerity of heart".*[206]

It is impossible to escape the evil that dwells witthin the unenlightened minds of sentient beings and the karmic environment they manifest, without the salvific Power of Amida Buddha. Until we reach His Pure Land we are never safe, and only after arriving there we are able to really benefit others.

*"The City of Bliss, tranquil and uncreated, in the West,
Is ultimately free and peaceful, far removed from being and nonbeing;
Transforming oneself into various bodies, one benefits all beings equally, without discrimination.*

*Let us return ! Do not abide
In this homeland of maras.*

---

[206] *Shan-tao's Liturgy for Birth – Ojoraisan*, compiled by Master Shan-tao, annotated translation by Zuio Hisao Inagaki, edited by Doyi Tan, Singapore, 2009, p.68

Since innumerable kalpas ago
We have been transmigrating
Passing through all the six courses.
Nowhere has there been any pleasure;
We hear only the voices of grief and sorrow.
After this present lifetime has ended,
Let us enter the city of Nirvana![207] "[208]

---

[207] Shinran Shonin explained, in his *Notes on the Inscriptions on Sacred Scrolls*: "'The city of Nirvana' is the Pure Land of peace. [...] Know that shinjin (faith in Amida Buddha) is the seed of Enlightenment, the seed for realizing the supreme Nirvana." *The Collected Works of Shinran*, Shin Buddhism Translation Series, Jodo Shinshu Hongwanji-ha, Kyoto, 1997, p.513

[208] Master Shan-tao as quoted by Shinran Shonin in his *Kyogyoshinsho*, chapter V, *The Collected Works of Shinran*, Shin Buddhism Translation Series, Jodo Shinshu Hongwanji-ha, Kyoto, 1997, p.200-201

The benefits of being born in the Pure Land of Amida Buddha

In order to help my Dharma companions to awake aspiration for the Pure Land, I will explain further the benefits of being born there. These should be read and contemplated in contrast with the previous descriptions of the sufferings of samsara, and with the rest of the *Four Thoughts that Turn the Mind Toward Amida Dharma*: the preciousness of human birth, impermanence and death, and karma - the law of cause and effect.

But before I enter into the details of this topic, we must remember a few key points. First of all, **the goal of Buddhism is to become a Buddha**. Not to paint this life in different colors, not to become a smart or interesting kind of Buddhist, but to become a Buddha. The Buddhist path is not a method of relaxation or a tablet for headache, something like "how can we become happier and calmer people" or a recipe for momentary happiness, but a road to Buddhahood or complete Freedom for us and all beings.

It is of utmost importance for those who enter the Buddhist path to have the aspiration to become a Buddha. Without this aspiration there is no Buddhism. If we don't want or don't feel the urgency of complete freedom from the many sufferings of repeated births and deaths, then Buddhism will remain for us only an object of study, an interesting lecture of mythology or an intellectual delight.

There are, so to speak, two visions one can have about himself and the world. The first is the ordinary vision depending on one's cultural education or daily concerns, and the other is the Dharmic vision.

The first represents what is considered normal in various times, containing limited explanations of the world and almost no interest in the meaning of human existence or in something which is beyond the present life. The immediate utilitarianism is fundamental in the non-Dharmic vision of the world.
On the other hand, the Dharmic vision perceives the world and personal life through the perspective of the Buddhist teaching (Dharma) where everything is explained in terms of the preciousness of human birth, impermanence, the law of karma, and the suffering inherent in all the samsaric realms of existence (the Four Thoughts). Also, what is truly important is defined in a different way than immediate utility, and the attainment of Freedom from samsara for us and all beings is considered to be supreme.

By reading, listening and deeply reflecting on the explanations offered by the Dharma about the world and our existence, one comes to understand why it is necessary to become a Buddha. By engaging more and more in the study of the Dharma, and by deeply understanding the Four Thoughts, we reach the point when we receive the so called, "Dharmic vision" or "Dharma eye". Then, many of our mental constructions that we considered to be solid and unbreakable will break down and the world will start to empty itself of the false colors projected on it and taken as the true reality.

Walking the Buddhist path with the aspiration to become a Buddha and having the Dharmic vision on our side, we become more intimate with our own karma, that is, we start to know ourselves better and especially our spiritual limitations. This stage – **the awareness of our spiritual limitations in comparison with the effort of becoming a Buddha** – is extremely important and especially emphasized in Jodo Shinshu. As I already explained in the various sections of the Four Thoughts, nothing is permanent in samsara, especially our so called "spiritual achievements". Thus, everything we think we attain now can be gone in the next hours, days or months, because our mental states are always changing. As death may come at any moment, we really do not have time for the so called "spiritual evolution" and the influence of our habitual karma from eons of living in the darkness of delusions and blind passions is always at work to hinder our most noble aspirations. When we reach the point where we wish to escape samsara, but realize it is impossible to do it through our own power and limited capacities, **we may become ready to accept Amida Buddha's helping hand** that is extended to us and all beings. If we listen deeply to Amida's simple message of salvation, entrust to Him, say His Name in faith and wish to be reborn in His Pure Land, we will finaly arrive at the end of our insane journey in samsara. This means that we become assured of birth in the Pure Land of Amida, and after we die we'll be reborn there and attain perfect Enlightenment.

By fully understanding the Four Thoughts as they were explained in this book, we easily come to accept the Three Pillars of Jodo Shinshu, that is, **1) we aspire to attain Buddhahood (perfect Enlightenment), 2) we realize our limitations and the imposibility of attaining this goal through our own power, and 3) we entrust to Amida Buddha in order to attain Buddhahood in His special Enlightened realm** where, unlike our samsaric environment, everything there is conducive to Enlightenment.

Faith (shinjin) as it is understood in Jodo Shinshu contains this twofold profound conviction (nishu jinshin): 1) we know that we are persons of deep karmic limitations, incapable to attain Buddhahood through our own power; and 2) we know that only Amida Buddha can save us through His Vow Power, without asking anything from us.

To aspire to become a Buddha is fundamental but this aspiration remains just an unfulfilled desire like many others if our personal capacities cannot lead us to this goal. It is not necessary to become a saint or some kind of special kind of person in order to have the aspiration to become a Buddha, but to be successful in attaining Buddhahood we'll need efforts and qualities infinitely greater than our ordinary capacities. So, in the moment we realize that **it is impossible** to attain this state through our own power, we are ready to hear the message of the Primal Vow of Amida Buddha.

It is very important to understand that Jodo Shinshu doesn't require to consider ourselves incapable in our daily activities, but only in matters of attaining supreme Liberation. To become a Buddha is not the same thing with being a good electrician, business man or anything we want in our private life. Such a difference should be very well discerned.

These being said, lets talk in more detail about the benefits of being born in the Pure Land.
Where do we learn about these benefits? First, from Amida Buddha himself as He promised in many of His vows[209] that we'll experience them after being born in His Pure Land. Second, from Shakyamuni Buddha who made great efforts to convince us about the existence of Amida Buddha and His Pure Land, by telling the story of Amida, describing His Enlightened Realm whenever He had the occasion, and by showing both of them to Ananda and the audience gathered on Vulture Peak. Third, from the Masters of our lineage and other lineages who also taught about the various benefits of being born there.

In order to show that people must accept the existence of Amida Buddha, and His Enlightened realm where we should aspire to be born, Shakyamuni Buddha revealed

---

[209] I explained in more detail all the 48 vows of Amida Buddha in my book, *The 48 Vows of Amida Buddha*, Dharma Lion Publications, Craiova, 2013. Also, the specific vows related with the capacities of beings born in the Pure Land are to be found at chapter III, p. 79- 92 of the same book, as well as page 66 where I explain the 22nd Vow.

them to His audience, when He taught the *Larger Sutra*. Here is what happened:

"The Buddha said to Ananda, 'Rise to your feet, rearrange your robes, put your palms together, and respectfully revere and worship Amitayus (Amida)[210].'
[...] Ananda stood up, rearranged his robes, assumed the correct posture, faced westward, and, demonstrating his sincere reverence, joined his palms together, prostrated himself on the ground, and worshiped Amitayus. Then he said to Śhakyamuni Buddha, 'World-honored One, I wish to see that Buddha, His Land of Peace and Bliss, and its hosts of bodhisattvas and sravakas'
As soon as he had said this, Amitayus emitted a great light, which illuminated all the Buddha lands. The Encircling Adamantine Mountains, Mount Sumeru, together with large and small mountains and everything else shone with the same [golden] color. That light was like the flood at the end of the period of cosmic change that fills the whole world, when myriads of things are submerged, and as far as the eye can see there is nothing but the vast expanse of water. Even so was the flood of light emanating from Amitayus. All the lights of sravakas and bodhisattvas were outshone and surpassed, and only the Buddha's light remained shining bright and glorious. At that time Ananda saw the splendor and majesty of Amitayus resembling Mount Sumeru, which rises above the whole world. There was no place that was not

---

[210] Amida Buddha has two aspects, "Infinite Life" (Amitayus) and "Infinite Light" (Amitabha). These two are merged into the word "Amida", which means the Buddha of Infinite Life and Infinite Light.

illuminated by the light emanating from His body of glory[211]. *The four groups of followers of the Buddha in the assembly saw all this at the same time. Likewise, those of the Pure Land saw everything in this world. Then the Buddha said to Ananda and Bodhisattva Maitreya, 'Have you seen that land filled with excellent and glorious manifestations, all spontaneously produced, from the ground to the Heaven of the Pure Abode?' Ananda replied, 'Yes, I have.' The Buddha asked, 'Have you also heard the great voice of Amitayus expound the Dharma to all the worlds, guiding sentient beings to the Way of the Buddha?' Ananda replied, 'Yes, I have.'"*[212]

The passage is clear and can't be misinterpreted. Ananda asked Shakyamuni to see Amida and His Pure Land - *"I wish to see that Buddha, His Land of Peace and Bliss"*, and then he actually saw Him – *"Ananda saw the splendor and majesty of Amitayus"*. In fact, not only him, but all those gathered there on Vulture Peak to listen to the *Larger Sutra*, saw Amida and the Pure Land – *"the four groups of followers of the Buddha in the assembly saw all this at the same time"*. Both those in this world

---

[211] Amida's Body of Glory is Sambhogakaya or Dharmakaya as compassionate means – Amida's transcendent body. For a detailed explanation, please read the chapter "The doctrine of the Three Buddha Bodies and Two Buddha Bodies in relation with Amida Buddha and His Pure Land" from my book, *The True Teaching on Amida Buddha and His Pure Land*, Dharma Lion Publications, Craiova, p.88

[212] *The Three Pure Land Sutras - A Study and Translation from Chinese* by Hisao Inagaki in collaboration with Harold Stewart, Bukkyo Dendo Kyokai and Numata Center for Buddhist Translation and Research, Kyoto, 2003, p.65-66

and those in the Pure Land, saw each other – *"likewise, those of the Pure Land saw everything in this world"*.

No sincere follower and reader of the above lines can possibly misinterpret what happened there. The revelation of Amida Buddha and His Land really took place, and the audience literally saw them before their very eyes. There is no hidden, metaphorical or symbolical meaning in this. I repeat, the audience literally saw them before their very eyes[213]. Anybody who tells you that you should not actually take into consideration this vision of Amida and His Land, as it was described in the sutra, is a person who lacks faith and who is consciously or unconsciously deceiving you, so please stay away from such people.

Not only that Shakyamuni showed Amida Buddha and the Pure Land to the audience, but He also asked them to confirm what they saw and heard:

"Have you seen that land filled with excellent and glorious manifestations, all spontaneously produced?"
To this, Ananda replied, "Yes, I have".
"Have you also heard the great voice of Amitayus?"
Ananda, also replied:
"Yes, I have".

---

[213] According to the *Contemplation Sutra*, Amida Buddha and His Pure Land were also shown to Queen Vaidehi, wife of King Bimbisara from Magadha. Ananda and Mahamaudgalyayana, two of His main disciples, were themselves present as witnesses of this revelation. For this, please go to page 82 from my book *The True Teaching on Amida Buddha and His Pure Land*, Dharma Lion Publications, Craiova, 2015.

Why do you think Shakyamuni Buddha asked them to confirm what they just saw and heard? Why He insisted to hear Ananda say with his own mouth, *"yes I have seen"* and *"yes, I have heard"*? It is because He wanted all beings, including us, disciples of later generations, to accept Amida as a real Buddha, and His Land as a real enlightened place where we should wish to go after death. It was for our sake that He told the story of Amida Buddha and enabled the audience to see Him and His Land:

"I have expounded this teaching (sutra) for the sake of sentient beings and enabled you to see Amitayus (Amida) and all in his Land. Strive to do what you should. After I have passed into Nirvana, do not allow doubt to arise."[214]

Not only Shakyamuni showed Amida Buddha and His Pure Land, but He described that Enlightened Realm whenever He had the occasion. For example, in the *Smaller Amida Sutra* (Amidakyo), Shakyamuni describes the Pure Land to Shariputra in an ecstatic manner not even giving time to His listener to ask questions. He starts preaching that sutra without being asked and He says on and on something like: "Shariputra, it is wonderful, that place is supreme in beauty…. Shariputra, in that land there are so and so places and so and so precious treasures…. Shariputra …….Shariputra…". It

---

[214] *The Three Pure Land Sutras - A Study and Translation from Chinese* by Hisao Inagaki in collaboration with Harold Stewart, Bukkyo Dendo Kyokai and Numata Center for Buddhist Translation and Research, Kyoto, 2003, p.70

seems that Shakyamuni doesn't even allow himself time to breathe when He speaks about the beauties of the Pure Land, such is His enthusiasm in presenting them.

Also, in order to show that Amida's Pure Land is not a metaphor, but a real place in which people can actually aspire to be born after death, the land is given a direction - the Pure Land of the West.

Some say that the direction "west" and the marvelous descriptions of the Pure Land are a proof for its non-existence or for its existence as a symbol or metaphor only. But the truth is that by making the effort to describe in many words the wonders of the Pure Land and by pointing to a direction where to face the Pure Land when worshipping Amida Buddha, Shakyamuni wants to emphasize its actual existence as a place where sentient beings should aspire to be born without worry and doubt.

It is as though I speak to you about a beautiful park I would like you to visit. If I tell you, "it's there, in the West part of town" and I start describing it to you, then you will have no doubt about its existence and you will wish to see it. It's the same with the expression "Pure Land of the West".

The exaltation with which Shakyamuni Buddha described the Pure Land of Amida in the *Smaller Amida Sutra (Amida-kyo)* without even being asked to do it (*Amidakyo* is a sutra spontaneously delivered, not in response to a question), or the radiant light that emanated from His body when He delivered the *Larger Sutra* in which He expounded the story of Amida and His 48th vows, are both an indication that His words were true and His listeners should accept Amida as a living Buddha and His Pure Land as a real place.

Again, in order to deny that the Pure Land is a real enlightened place with forms and manifestations, and stop you from awakening the true aspiration to be born there, some would try to present the Pure Land only as a state of consciousness. But you should not be fooled by them, because **states of consciousness do not exclude forms and manifestations!** In fact, depending on the states of consciesness one dwells in, various forms appear. Thus, for unenlightened beings, samsaric bodies and realms come into existence as effects of their specific karmic obscurations. When one becomes a Buddha, transcendental manifestations arise as the effect of Enlightenment and the wish to save all beings.

There will always be forms and manifestations, no matter we are enlightened or unenlightened. When unenlightened conditions are present, unenlightened forms which lead to more attachments and blind passions, appear. When Enlightenment is present, enlightened forms or manifestations appear - this is why all Buddhas assume various trancendent bodies and create special spheres of influence which are called Pure Lands.

Buddhas do not depend on forms and their minds are always free of forms, but this does not mean they reject forms. Only deluded practitioners can fall in the wrong view of attachement to emptiness and negate forms, saying that everything, including the Pure Land is just a state of mind.

In our samsaric world everything is the effect of our unenlightened karma and so, we live in a garden of never ending desires and suffering. Contrary to this, the Pure Land is the effect or the manifestation of Amida Buddha's Enlightenment and of His wish to save all beings. Thus, e**verything there is conducive to Enlightenment**. Shakyamuni Buddha clearly explained the Pure Land of Amida as a real place with various forms which He insisted that they are not the product of unenlightened karma, but the manifestations of Amida. For example, describing the birds in the Pure Land, Shakyamuni Buddha said:

"Shariputra, you should not assume that these birds are born as retribution of their evil karma. The reason is that none of the three evil realms exists in that Buddha-land. Shariputra, even the names of the three evil realms do not exist there; how much less the realms themselves? ***These birds are manifested by Amida Buddha*** *so that their singing can proclaim and spread the Dharma".*[215]

This clearly shows that the Pure Land is both an existing place and a place of Enlightenment.

The foundation of samsara is ignorance and blind passions; the foundation (essence) of the Pure Land is Nirvana or Perfect Enlightenment. **Both ignorance and**

---

[215] The *Larger Sutra*.

Enlightenment are accompanied by forms. Ignorance and blind passions give rise to various samsaric realms, while perfect Enlightenment manifest Pure Lands. Thus, the Pure Land of Amida Buddha is the effect of His Enlightenment and the wish to save all beings as expressed in His 48 Vows. This is the right teaching on the Pure Land.

If somebody tells you that the Pure Land is only a state of consciousness or that it is only a place, he is not teaching the true Dharma. The first is a variant of the wrong view of "nihilistic voidness" and "attachment to emptiness", while the second is the wrong view of considering the Pure Land as a mere place of samsara.
Again, the right way to define the Pure Land in our human language is - **the enlightened realm of Amida Buddha.**

It is extremely important to understand that manifestations, from the hells to the Pure Land, come into existence due to causes and conditions. If you have a karma so evil that you deserve to be born into hell, you will be born there; if you have the karma to be born as human you will be born as a human, and so on… Just like unenlightened beings karmically manifest unenlightened realms with various pains and obstacles, a Buddha manifests an Enlightened Realm. If in the first case, the manifestations in unenlightened realms are conducive to more attachments and delusions, in the Pure Land of Amida Buddha there are enlightened manifestations and forms which lead to Enlightenment.

As we have seen above, in Shakyamuni's explanations, the birds of the Pure Land are not the result, like in our realm, of an unenlightened karma, but are manifested by Amida Buddha. If in the hells, various birds and terrifying beasts prey on the hell dwellers because those birds and beasts are the effect of the karma of hell dwellers, in the Pure Land the various birds sing Dharma music and speak about Nirvanic truths because they are manifested from Amida's Enlightenment. Both animals (those of hell and the Pure Land) are real, **but they exist due to different causes. The beasts from hell have the cause in an unenlightened karma (the karma of hell dwellers), while the second have their cause in Amida's Enlightenment**, and in Bodhisattva Dharmakara's[216] Vows which were brought to fulfillment when He became Amida Buddha.

The joys and pleasures of those born in the Pure Land do not come from attachement to senses or sense objects, but from Enlightenment and the enlightened nature of that realm. Thus, they go beyond any pleasure of the gods or unenlightened superior beings. As Master Genshin said:

"Even the pleasures of the hundred million thousand years of life in Toriten[217] or the pleasures of the deep

---

[216] Before He became a Buddha, Amida was called Dharmakara. Please read the chapter, "The story of Amida Buddha as told by Shakyamuni Buddha", from my book, *The True Teaching on Amida Buddha and His Pure Land*, Dharma Lion Publications, Craiova, p.66

[217] Toriten, the second of the Six Devalokas.

ecstasies of Mahabrahman's palace are not to be regarded as pleasures in comparison with these pleasures of the Pure Land. When the karma of reward is exhausted the one living in Toriten or Mahabrahman's palace falls at last again into the cycle of change and he cannot escape from the three evil realms[218], but this one who has been born into the Pure Land is now resting thankfully in the arms of Kannon (Avalokitesvara Bodhisttva)[219] and he is dwelling securely on the Treasure Lotus Seat[220]. Having passed a long period of time in crossing the Sea of Suffering, he has now for the first time been born into the Pure Land, and his happiness is thus beyond the power of words to describe."

In His 32nd Vow, Amida Buddha made the following promise about His Pure Land:

"If, when I attain Buddhahood, all the myriads of manifestations in my land, from the ground to the sky, such as palaces, pavilions, ponds, streams and trees, should not be composed of both countless treasures, which surpass in supreme excellence anything in the worlds of humans and devas, and of a hundred thousand

---

[218] The three evil realms are hell, realm of hungry ghosts and animal realm.

[219] Avalokitesvara and Mahasthamaprapta are the two Enlightened Bodhisattvas who accompany Amida Buddha in His Pure Land, helping all beings, in various ways, to entrust to Amida and be born there.

[220] One who was born in the Pure Land through the gate of faith is secured in his attainment of perfect Enlightenment. The "treasure lotus seat" is the throne of Enlightenment.

kinds of aromatic wood, whose fragrance pervades all the worlds of the ten quarters, causing all bodhisattvas who sense it to perform Buddhist practices, then may I not attain perfect Enlightenment."[221]

These transcendent manifestations also show that the Pure Land surpasses all other places in the world of suffering – *"surpass in supreme excellence anything in the worlds of humans and devas"*.

In fact, the Pure Land is beyond samsara and cannot be compared with the realms caught in the power of birth and death, thus subject to impermanence. Humans, devas (gods) plus other kinds of sentient beings and the environment in which they are born are the product of their unenlightened karma, but the Pure Land of Amida is the manifestation of His supreme Enlightenment and pure merits, so all its treasures and manifestations are supreme in beauty while in the same time they have the power to deepen and strengthen the dedication of those engaged in the practice of liberating themselves and others (bodhisattvas):

"a hundred thousand kinds of aromatic wood, whose fragrance pervades all the worlds of the ten quarters, causing all bodhisattvas who sense it to perform Buddhist practices."

---

[221] *The Three Pure Land Sutras - A Study and Translation from Chinese* by Hisao Inagaki in collaboration with Harold Stewart, Bukkyo Dendo Kyokai and Numata Center for Buddhist Translation and Research, Kyoto, 2003, p.18

Again, it is clear that the treasures found in the Pure Land are not intended for the enjoyment of the six senses but for expressing the Dharma, calling beings to the Dharma, praising Amida's virtues and showing the supreme place this enlightened land occupies among other Buddha lands. They are spiritual treasures, even if they are described using the terms we are familiar with, like *palaces, pavilions, ponds, streams and trees, aromatic wood,* etc.

*

Certainly, the most important benefit of birth in the Pure Land through the Gate of Faith is the attainment of Nirvana or complete Buddhahood:

"When a person has entered completely into the Pure Land of happiness, he or she immediately realizes the supreme Nirvana; he realizes the supreme Enlightenment".[222]

From this benefit, all other benefits emerge like branches of a tree. Thus, **once we become Buddhas in the Pure Land, we'll have access to the ultimate reality beyond form (Dharmakaya), we'll dwell forever in transcendent form (Sambhogakaya) in Amida's Pure Land, and in the same time we'll go in all the places of the universe in various Bodies of Accomodation or Transformation (Nirmanakayas) to save all**

---

[222] Shinran Shonin, *Lamp for the Latter-Ages*, letter 21, *The Collected Works of Shinran*, Shin Buddhism Translation Series, Jodo Shinshu Hongwanji-ha, Kyoto, 1997, p.555

beings. The promise of attaining Buddhahood and returning to help all beings was made by Amida Buddha in His 11th[223] and 22nd Vow[224] respectivelly.

Because in the Pure Land we'll be dwelling in Nirvana, we'll have *"noble and majestic countenance, unequaled in all the worlds"* and our appearance will be *"superb, unmatched by any being, heavenly or human"*. We'll be *"endowed with bodies of Naturalness, Emptiness, and Infinity."*[225]

To have the body of Naturalness, Emptiness and Infinity, is surely a proof that we'll attain Buddhahood or supreme Enlightenment (Nirvana). Shinran Shonin also said:

"Their countenances are dignified and wonderful, surpassing things of this world. Their features, subtle and delicate, are not those of human beings or devas; all receive the body of naturalness or of emptiness, the body of boundlessness."[226]

---

[223] See my detailed explanations of the 11th Vow in my book *The 48 Vows of Amida Buddha*, Dharma Lion Publications, Craiova, 2013, p. 57

[224] See my detailed explanations of the 22nd Vow in my book *The 48 Vows of Amida Buddha*, Dharma Lion Publications, Craiova, 2013, p. 66

[225] Shakyamuni Buddha, *Larger Sutra* in The *Three Pure Land Sutras*, translated by Hisao Inagaki in collaboration with Harold Stewart, revised second edition, Numata Center for Buddhist Translation and Research, Berkeley, California, 2003, p.31

[226] *The Collected Works of Shinran*, Shin Buddhism Translation Series, Jodo Shinshu Hongwanji-ha, Kyoto, 1997, p.300

Amida Buddha promised in His 3rd Vow that we'll have *"the color of pure gold"* while in His 4th Vow He said we'll *"be of one appearance"*, without *"any difference in beauty"*.
As we know, unenlightened samsaric beings have various forms and shapes, color and beauty, being very different from one another due to the different types of karma they inherit from past lives. But once we are born in the Pure Land and become Buddhas we are liberated from the shackles of karma and go beyond form, color and any differences. This is what is meant by *"all be of one appearance"*. To be of the color of pure gold also means to have transcendent bodies of the qualities of Enlightenment.

Bodhisattva Nagarjuna said:

'In Amida's infinite and accommodating realm there is no bad purpose or foolish wisdom. There is no illumination in evil causes but only natural progress in the Buddha Way. ***If one obtains birth there he will be unmoved and he will attain full Enlightenment.****"*[227]
In His 21st Vow Amida Buddha promised that after birth in His Pure Land we'll be *"endowed with the thirty-two physical characteristics of a Great Man"*. Shakyamuni Buddha too, said the same in the *Larger Sutra*:

"Ananda, the sentient beings born there all fully posses the thirty two physical characteristics of a Great Man as well as perfect wisdom, with which they penetrate deeply

---

[227] A poem by Bodhisattva Nagarjuna as quoted by Master Genshin in his *Ojoyoshu*.

into the nature of all dharmas[228] and reach their subtle essence. Their supernatural powers know no obstruction and their physical senses are sharp and clear".[229]

Master Genshin also said:

"The beings in the Pure Land, having bodies of golden color and being pure inwardly and outwardly, give forth a brilliant light and thus mutually glorify each other. They have thirty-two forms and they are so sublime, upright and marvelous that there is nothing with which to compare them in this world. [...] If we should compare the masters of the Six Devalokas[230] with the beings of the Pure Land it would be like a beggar standing alongside of a king."

In His 15th Vow Amida Buddha promised that we'll have unlimited life-spans[231], which means that our Sambhogakaya (transcendent) body in the Pure Land will have no end, and that we will forever manifest in various forms (Nirmanakayas) all over samsara to save beings, maintaining those manifestations as long as we wish. Actually, **as Enlightened ones, we'll go beyond birth**

---

[228] When the word "dharma" is used with small "d" it refers to all existence and phenomena in general. When its used with "D" like in "Dharma" it means the Buddha's teaching.
[229] *Three Pure Land Sutras*, translated by Hisao Inagaki in collaboration with Harold Stewart, revised second edition, Numata Center for Buddhist Translation and Research, Berkeley, California, 2003, p.41-42
[230] Six realms of samsaric existence.
[231] Those born in the Pure Land are beyond death, so their bodies of manifestations have unlimited life span.

and death, so we can be in the Pure Land and in other worlds at the same time.

In His 5th Vow, Amida Buddha promised that after being born in the Pure Land we'll remember *"all previous lives"* and know *"the events which occurred during the previous hundred thousand kotis of nayutas of kalpas"*, while in the 6th Vow He promised we'll *"possess the divine eye of seeing even a hundred thousand kotis of nayutas of Buddha-lands"*. In the 8th Vow He assured us that we'll have *"the faculty of knowing the thoughts of others"*, and in the 9th Vow that we'll be able to go *"anywhere in one instant, even beyond a hundred thousand kotis of nayutas of Buddha-lands"* so that we can always be together with any being we want to help.

Master Genshin said:

"As those born in the Pure Land have power to understand their own destinies, they talk to each other about their former lives, namely, as to what country they lived in, how their mind became enlightened by this and that scripture when they were seeking the way of the Buddha, how they kept this and that precept, and learned such and such teachings and thus developed the Good Root, and how they gave such and such alms. In this way they talk with one another about the virtues which they enjoyed, or they tell in detail the story from beginning to end of how they came to be born into the Pure Land."
[...]

The various beings of the Pure Land have all the five mysterious communications whose marvelous nature cannot be comprehended. They live a life of freedom according to their heart's desire. If, for example, they wish to look across the universe without taking a step they can do so. If they wish to hear the voice of anyone in the universe they can do so without moving from their seats. Not only this, but they can hear also the things of the infinite past as if they were happening today. They know the inmost thoughts of the beings of the six realms as if they were reflected in a mirror. They can go and come freely as if all the lands of the Buddha in all the ten directions lay beneath their feet. They can do anything they please in the realm of infinite space and in the realm of endless time. [...]

For beings in our world it is impossible to see without sun light or lamp-light; and, without moving, it is impossible to approach an object. We cannot see through even one sheet of paper. We know nothing of the things in the past; we know merely the things of the present moment. We are still confined to the cage and obstructed in every direction. But as for the beings in the Pure Land there is not one which does not have this power (of mysteriously transcending space and time). Even though for a period of a hundred Great Kalpas they have not planted the seed (karma) of the Special Characteristic Forms and have not created the cause for the Mysterious Communications, during the Four Meditations, **they still have this power as a natural consequence of having been born into the Pure Land**. *How happy, then, they must be!"*.

He also said:

"The things men seek after while living in this world are not really in accordance with their hearts' desires. The tree seeks to be quiet but the wind blows without ceasing. The son wishes to take care of his parents but the parents do not survive long enough. And even though the parents should live, the son, in the case of a poor family, cannot provide what his filial piety would prompt him to do even though he would be ready to 'burst his bladder' in the attempt. If he goes far away from home or business he will be unable to look upon the graceful faces of his parents in the morning or care for them in the bedchamber in the evening. As all this is impossible for him, he breaks his heart in vain in the effort. The same thing is true in the relationship of master and servant, teacher and disciple, husband and wife, friend and friends, among relatives and with all people, to whom one owes an obligation. By worrying thus with a heart of foolish love one only increases the work of karma.

Every man knows where he is now and what kind of life he is living in the six realms and the four births. But who knows that the animal in the field or the bird on the mountain may not once have been our parents in their former existence. This thought is expressed in an old poem which reads: 'There is a cuckoo in the hillside field crying 'Cuckoo! Cuckoo!' Who knows but that it is my father or my mother.' In a verse of the Shindikwagyo we read: 'Men in this world commit various sins for the sake of their children and then they fall down into the realms of hell, hungry spirits or animals to receive suffering for a long time. Not being saints nor having the mysterious power of communication they cannot understand their former transmigrations. All beings fail to make retribution by kindness to others. All beings are caught on the wheel of birth and death. They pass around from stage to stage in the six realms like the wheel of a wagon, without beginning or end. At one time they are father or mother, at another time may be husband or wife, and they show kindness to each other during the various lives in this world. But if they are born into the Pure Land they are endowed with a superior wisdom and their clear power of mysterious communication reaches unto those who were formerly their benefactors and to those who were their acquaintances through many lives and generations, they can attract them freely. Endowed with a heavenly eye, they can see where they live, and with their heavenly ear they can hear their voice. Their wisdom of destiny enables them to remember the favors (of their former benefactors) and with their insight into others' hearts they understand their hearts. Their mysterious powers of communication enable them to go where they are, and by changing their form they can adapt themselves to their needs and in various ways teach them and lead them in the way of salvation."

In the 7th Vow Amida Buddha promised that we'll have the *"divine ear of hearing the teachings of at least a hundred thousand kotis of nayutas of Buddhas"* and *"remember all of them"*, that we'll directly worship all Buddhas in all the ten directions (24th Vow), make offerings to them (23rd Vow), and hear spontaneously whatever teachings we may wish (the 46th Vow).

Master Genshin said:

"While believers are still in this present world, seeing and hearing through the scriptures about the various virtues of the Buddha lands of the Ten Directions, they beget a heart of longing and they say sadly to each other: 'When shall we be able to see the pure lands of the ten directions and meet with the various Buddhas and Bodhisattvas?' But if one should by chance obtain birth into this Pure Land one can go in the morning and return in the evening or go and come in a moment to and from all the Buddha lands which lie in the ten directions. There one may serve the various Buddhas, live with the great teachers and continually hear about the true Dharma. Such a one obtains entrance into the perfect Enlightenment. Moreover, such a one can enter the various mundane spheres, engage in the various Buddhist ceremonies and practice works of benevolence. Is not this real joy?"

Not only that we'll be able to go to other realms to worship, make offerings and listen to the teachings of other Buddhas, but many saints and Enlightened beings will also come to the Pure Land to pay homage to Amida, so we'll be able to meet them there!
Master Genshin said:

"As it is said in the Scriptures, 'All beings who hear of these pleasures rouse a desire to be born into this Land. That is because they can meet in fellowship with the various people of the highest good.' The virtues of the hosts of Bodhisattvas are wonderful."

Then he mentioned the names of various Enlightened Bodhisattvas we can meet in the Pure Land, among which there are, Samantabhadra, Manjushri, Maitreya, Ksitigarbha, Avalokitesvara, Mahasthamaprapta, etc

He also said:

"The great Bodhisattvas are numberless like the grains of sand on the Ganges river. Their color and form is beautiful and they are full of virtue. They live continually in the Pure Land and gather about Amida Nyorai. [...] The Pure Land is filled with a throng of holy beings who have a common life, see each other and hear each other's voice and who seek after the same way. There is no difference among them. There are numberless beings and Bodhisattvas from the Buddha lands of the ten directions, as numerous as the grains of sand on the Ganges river. Each one of these reveals his mysterious power of communication and comes to the Pleasant Country (Pure Land) where he looks upon the precious face of Amida Nyorai and makes offerings to Him in reverence. Some of them make offerings of wonderful heavenly flowers, some burn a wonderful kind of incense, and some offer priceless garments. There are some who make heavenly music and praise the Nyorai with soft and calm voices. Some listen to the scriptures or propagate the teaching. There is no hindrance in their going and coming night and day. Some go away to the east while others are coming from the west. Some go away to the west while others are coming from the north. And again some return to the north while others are coming from the south. Thus the throngs come and go from the four corners, the eight

directions and the directions up and down. **It is like a flourishing marketplace.** *To hear once the names of such saints does not happen by accident. How much more likely then, must it be to meet with one through the hundred, thousand, ten thousand kalpas! And the beings in the Pure Land gather together continually in one place and talk with each other, exchange stories, ask questions, act with prudence, respect and are friendly toward one another and become intimate with each other. Is this not real enjoyment?*

Nagarjuna said, 'The various children of Buddha, coming from the ten directions, reveal clearly the mysterious power of communication. They behold the precious form of Amida and do Him reverence continually. Therefore I bow down before Amida Nyorai and worship Him.'"

We will also never *"give rise to thoughts of self-attachment"* as promised by Amida Buddha in His 10th Vow. To be free of self attachment is to go beyond limited visions of "I and others", to perceive all beings with equanimity and non-discrimination. This is the same of having understood emptiness of all phenomena. Shakyamuni Buddha said in the *Larger Sutra* about those born in the Pure Land:

"Whether going or coming, proceeding or remaining, their hearts are unattached, their acts are in accordance with their will and are unrestricted, and they have no thought of discrimination. In them there is no idea of self or others, no idea of compensation or dispute. With the heart of great Compassion to benefit all living beings and

with tenderness and self-control, they bear no enmity or grudge against anyone. Free of mental hindrances, they are pure in mind and without indolence. [...] Their samsaric bodies and evil passions have been extinguished together with their remaining karmic tendencies. [...]Their wisdom is like the ocean, and their Samadhi, like the king of mountains. [....They are like the great earth, because they have no discriminative thoughts, such as pure or impure, beautiful or ugly. [...] They are like the sky, because they have no attachments. [...] They are like a flock of playful birds, because they do not store things. [....] They are like the vast sky, because their great Compassion reaches everywhere without discrimination.

They have destroyed envy by not being jealous of the superiority of others. [...] Thus they become lamps to the world and fields of supreme merit; they always become teachers and harbor no thought of discrimination, aversion or attachment".[232]

According to the 16th Vow, no wrongdoing will be found in us after we attain Buddhahood in the Pure Land, no ignorance and blind passions, but only perfect hapiness as also promised in the 39th Vow. Thus, because of the absence of ignorance and blind passions, in the Pure Land there are no lower realms (1st Vow) and no so

---

[232] *Three Pure Land Sutras*, translated by Hisao Inagaki in collaboration with Harold Stewart, revised second edition, Numata Center for Buddhist Translation and Research, Berkeley, California, 2003, p.43-44

called "higher realms", and once born there we'll never fall again in samsaric existence (2nd Vow).

According to the 25th Vow, 29th, and the 30th Vow, we will have unsurpassed and *"all-knowing wisdom"* for instructing beings everywhere in accordance with their capacities. More than this, we'll be *"endowed with the body of the Vajra-god Narayana"* (26th Vow). Vajra- god Narayana is in fact Vajrapani (from Sanskrit vajra, "thunderbolt" or "diamond" and pani, lit. "in the hand"), one of the most important Enlightened Bodhisattvas[233] of Mahayana Buddhism. He is the protector of Buddha Dharma, and He represents the Power of all Buddhas.

---

[233] There are two types of bodhisattvas:

1. Ordinary type of bodhisattvas in aspiration who make the vows of becoming Buddhas for themselves and all beings, but who are still on the path and still unenlightened (not Buddhas yet). Anyone who now makes the above Bodhisattva vows may call himself or herself a bodhisattva in aspiration.

and

2. Bodhisattvas who already attained Buddhahood or perfect Enlightenment but who do not remain secluded in this Enlightenment. These are in fact, Buddhas who manifest themselves as Bodhisattvas.

Those who are born in the Pure Land of Amida through the gate of the Primal Vow become such Buddhas who manifest themselves as Bodhisattvas. Avalokitesvara, Vajrapani, Mahasthamaprapta, Samantabhadra, etc fall into the category of Enlightened Bodhisattvas. Please carefully read my explanations in the chapter "Returning from the Pure Land - explanation of the 22nd Vow" from *The 48 Vows of Amida Buddha*, Dharma Lion Publications, Craiova, p. 66 and my article *On the Buddhas who Manifest as Bodhisattvas* from http://amida-ji-retreat-temple-romania.blogspot.ro/2016/09/on-bodhisattvas-who-became-buddhas-but.html

Just as Samantabhadra Bodhisattva, mentioned in the 22nd Vow, represents the endless saving activity of all Buddhas, Vajrapani represents the immense and all surpassing Power of the Buddhas. After birth in the Pure Land, we'll be exactly like these two Enlightened Bodhisattvas. Just like Samantabhadra, we'll always be active in samsara, and like Vajrapani, we'll be all-powerful. And because Vajrapani is a protector of the Dharma, we will also become Dharma protectors and destroyers of wrong views.

Concluding verses on the Four Profound Thoughts which turn the mind towards Amida Dharma

I take refuge in Amida Buddha, my unfailing and constant protector!
This precious human birth is difficult to obtain.
My body and my so called "spiritual achievements" are impermanent and cannot be trusted.
Virtuous and non-virtuous actions bring their inevitable results,
and the influence of past habitual karma makes it impossible to attain Buddhahood in this life.
The six planes of existence are an ocean of suffering and escape is impossible by relying on self power.
Recognizing this, may my mind turn towards Amida Dharma.

Namo Amida Bu

Rev Jōshō Adrian Cîrlea is the representative of Jodo Shinshu Buddhist Community from Romania, founder of Tariki Dojo and Amidaji temple.

Printed in Great Britain
by Amazon